WHAT ABOUT US WHO ARE NOT HEALED ?

WHAT ABOUT US WHO ARE NOT HEALED

?

Carmen Benson

Logos International
Plainfield, New Jersey

Scripture quotations are taken from the King James Version of the Bible unless otherwise identified. Symbols for other versions quoted are:

AP - Author's paraphrase.

ASV - American Standard Version, © 1929 by the International Council of Religious Education. Published by the American Bible Society, New York.

RSV - Revised Standard Version, © 1952 by Division of Christian Education of the National Council of the Churches of Christ in the United States of America.

SCO - The New Scofield Reference Bible, © 1967 by Oxford University Press, New York.

Library of Congress Catalog Card Number: 75-2800
International Standard Book Number: 0-88270-112-6 (cloth)
0-88270-113-4 (paper)

Grateful Acknowledgment
to
Paulist Press, New York, N.Y.
"The Life of St. Teresa" translated by David Lewis published 1962, Newman Press, Westminster, Maryland
Rev. Ray Schoch, founder and pastor of Faith Center, Glendale, California—personal interview

This book is dedicated to
those I love, who long have had to suffer with me;
and to
my Blessed Lord,
the most longsuffering of all.

Contents

Part Two—The Cure

Preface

A *prescription*, written by a physician, is for the preparation of a medicine. The prescription is to be filled and taken as directed.

An *inscription*, written at the beginning of every chapter in this book, is for the preparation and use of the reader. Take one tablet before each message. Chew thoroughly, or allow to dissolve in the mind. Aids digestion of contents.

Chapter titles contain formula used. Read labels carefully.

Active ingredients of *capsules preceding Part One and Part Two* were compounded from Webster's dictionary and from God's pharmacy, the Bible. Swallow slowly. Do not exceed recommended dosage. Follow with a full glass of the water of life.

Caution: This preparation should be used with care by persons suffering from spiritual high blood pressure, hardening of the doctrines, or closed-mind disease. If these symptoms persist, consult the Great Physician at once.

What About Us Who Are Not Healed?

I can hear someone say, "Oh that's a book about weaklings, written by a weakling." My friend, you are absolutely right— But did you know that *you* are one of the weaklings?

All of us are weaklings, because we all have our weaknesses— of one kind or another. If you think you are an exception, that very thought betrays two of your biggest weaknesses—pride, and blindness to self.

But take heart. Remember, the Lord told Paul that His strength was made perfect in weakness. To which that great apostle of faith replied, "Most gladly therefore will I glory in my weaknesses, that the power of Christ may rest upon me" (II Cor. 12:9 sco).

While Paul's weaknesses (infirmities) are, of course, different from ours, the Bible promises us the Holy Spirit's help in our particular weaknesses (Rom. 8:26). The Scripture also tells us that Jesus, our great High Priest, understands and has compassion on us in our weaknesses (Heb. 4:15). And both the Spirit and the Son of God make intercession for us. How marvelous!

Yes, "those of us who are not healed" means you as well as me. I don't care how good your physical health is. You may be a rugged specimen of vitality, without an ache or a pain or an ailment of any kind. You may never have known a sick day in your life. But you are not healed in the true meaning of the word.

You are not "healed" in God's sight. And possibly you are sicker spiritually, mentally, or emotionally than some poor sufferer lying in a hospital bed, whose body is torn to pieces with pain and disease.

I can imagine the reaction of many as they read these words. Somebody is sputtering: "Who does she think she is, saying such a thing? The Bible plainly states: 'With his stripes we are healed' (Isa. 53:5; I Pet. 2:24). Besides that, there's nothing wrong with me. I'm not sick physically, mentally, emotionally or spiritually. The Lord has saved me, baptized me, filled me, healed me, used me, justified me, sanctified me—and when I die, He will glorify me. There's something wrong with her all right, but not with me!"

First of all, the word "heal" comes from the root word "whole." To be healed literally means "to be made whole." What does it mean to be made whole? Webster defines it as being: "complete, perfect, the omitting or abating of nothing—entire— a perfection from which nothing has been taken and to which nothing can be added."

Now, even in the eyes of the dictionary, who among us could boast of wholeness—that he is complete, having everything, perfect in every way, coming short in nothing?

And certainly in the eyes of God, who could boast? What's more, in God's sight, if you are spiritually whole, you are holy. The root meaning of "holy" comes from the same word that means "whole." You are of unimpaired innocence and proved virtue. You are perfect.

"Nobody is perfect," I can hear someone interject. "God doesn't expect us to be perfect."

Doesn't He?

Jesus flatly charged His disciples in the Sermon on the Mount:"Be ye therefore perfect, even as your Father which is in heaven is perfect" (Matt. 5:48). And that qualifying phrase "as your Father which is in heaven is perfect" leaves no room for misinterpretation of the standard or the scope of perfection.

I am aware that the Greek word translated here as "perfect" means "completed, to have reached maturity, fully developed in mental and moral character," while the word used for "holy"means "sacred, pure, morally blameless, consecrated."

But since God has predestinated us to be conformed to the image of His Son, how could we be completed, fully matured and developed in Christian character, without being sacred (set apart in honor of and as dear to God), pure, morally blameless, and consecrated? They are inseparable. That is why personal holiness is commanded by God in both the Old and New Testaments (Lev. 11:44; I Pet. 1:15,16; II Pet. 3:11).

Paul very clearly declared that God's people are divinely intended to "come . . . unto a perfect man, unto the measure of the stature of the fulness of Christ" (Eph. 4:13) that they might "stand perfect and complete in all the will of God" (Col. 4:12).

Let me ask you a few direct questions:

Have you fulfilled the many injunctions God gave through Moses that His people must be holy, separated from all uncleanness, sin, and immoral living, and consecrated to the same end in life to which God is consecrated? Do you measure up to the stature of the fullness of Christ? Do you stand perfect and complete in all the will of God?

A man whom my husband and I have known for thirty years—unregenerate by Bible standards, a plain garden-variety sinner, albeit a good man by the world's criteria—sat in our living room and solemnly asserted that not only was he a good man (who didn't need the Bible, the church, or the Lord Jesus Christ as Savior), but that he was "holy."

Aghast, I asked him if he knew what the word "holy" meant. "Would you say that you are on a par with God, 'worthy of adoration or veneration'?" I asked him in shocked tones.

He thought for a moment, then replied in all sincerity, "Yes, I would."

As if that weren't incredible enough, his wife spoke up and said that she agreed with him! She also would label him as "holy."

Now, you may not go so far as to consider yourself holy and perfect. But if—in the light of these definitions and Scriptures—you still think that you do not need healing in some area of your life (physical, mental, emotional, or spiritual), then you have absolutely nothing more to attain. You are a finished product.

To the rest of us—those who admit we need some kind of healing which so far we have not realized—and especially to those who are suffering daily and wondering what has happened to God's restorative power—I offer the following pages as one woman's experience with the Holy Spirit regarding this important question, *What About Us Who Are Not Healed?*

Part One — The Complaint

Webster defines complaint:

"Expression of grief, pain, or resentment. An ailment. Sickness. Disease. A formal allegation against a party."

David complains:

"I cried unto the LORD with my voice. . . . I Poured out my complaint before him; I showed before him my trouble. I am desolate and afflicted. . . . Look upon mine affliction and my pain" (Ps. 142:1,2 SCO Ps. 25:16,18).

Job also complains:

"I will give free utterance to my complaint; I will speak in the bitter of my soul. I will say to God, Do not condemn me; let me know why thou dost contend against me" (Job 10:1,2 RSV).

I

"This Sickness Is Not unto Death"

(John 11:4)

I said, "I have awful pain in my stomach."
The doctor said, "At the opening of your stomach is an
hiatal hernia, and where your stomach empties is a
duodenal ulcer."
Jesus said, "Out of your belly shall flow rivers of living
water." (John 7:38 AP).

I begin this book sitting up in bed, sipping warm half-and-half
to ease my stomach pain, a heating pad covering as much of my
hurting places as it will reach, and thinking about two phone
calls of the morning.

The first was a long-distance call from Dr. Ray Charles
Jarman in Arlington, Virginia . . . Dear Dr. Jarman—my former
pastor, my "boss" for the many years I was his secretary in the
church he founded, co-author of the first book either of us
published, and the one earthly friend I have turned to again and
again over the past quarter of a century.

"Carmen," he began, after inquiring about my physical condition, "I have something important to say to you."

"What is it?" I asked listlessly, for nothing was very important to me, short of an instant miracle to heal all that ailed me.

"I have had a revelation regarding you," he stated with assurance and a degree of excitement. "Last night a very earnest group of us met in prayer, and we prayed for you. It was clearly revealed to me that you are going to write another book, and it is going to be about suffering."

"Suffering!" I gasped incredulously. Then with a weak laugh I said, "Well, that's one subject I wouldn't have to do any research on. That is the story of my life! But you know as well as I that I'll never write another book."

Ignoring this, he continued. "Before you can do anything," he said, "one thing is essential. You have got to give up this death-wish that you have been harboring for so long! You can never be healed or fulfill God's will for your life as long as that is present." His manner was stern, yet kind—even entreating.

"Look," I responded wearily, "I can bear suffering for a while, but after years of it—pain heaped upon pain, with never a day of respite—I find it just too much! Surely that cannot be God's will for anyone!"

He didn't reply, so I resumed my line of self-defense. "No one—not even an animal—who is wounded and in pain and caught in a trap from which there is no escape save death, could help but long for release. You would have to be out of your mind to want to stay there!"

Undaunted, he declared, "That death-wish of yours comes from an evil spirit. We have rebuked it in the name of the Lord Jesus Christ! But you," he paused to emphasize his next words, "must of your own free will cease giving in to it."

I said nothing for a moment, but I was thinking, Such a wish does not seem evil to me. In fact, it seems to make perfect spiritual sense. It is scriptural. "Having a desire to depart, and to be with Christ . . . is far better" (Phil. 1:23), wrote the apostle Paul. "To die is gain" (Phil. 1:21). Even the great prophet Elijah petitioned God that he might die. "It is enough now, O LORD , take away my life" (I Kings 19:4), he prayed. . . . And he wasn't even

4

sick, or in pain!

Job, who really was in misery, also prayed for death. "Oh that I might have my request; and that God would grant me the thing that I long for! Even that it would please God to destroy me; that he would let loose his hand, and cut me off! Then I should yet have comfort" (Job 6:8-10).

Countless were the supplications of David to be delivered from his affliction, pain, and trouble on this earth. No doubt there were other death-wishes recorded in the Bible. Not to mention some that were thought or prayed without any record being made of them.

These examples seemed more than sufficient to justify my longing to have done with this life. I had spent over fifty years here, most of them blighted by intermittent or continual physical suffering, weakness, toil, disappointment, and disillusionment.

Oh, certainly there had been good things, too—beauty, spiritual joy, serenity, and love. But at this point in my life, I was too old, too tired, too ravaged by circumstance, too full of self-pity to see anything wrong with wanting to take my leave and go to the heaven we Christians hold as the goal of our existence. I was also too weak to continue the argument with Dr. Jarman.

"You may be right," I conceded grudgingly. "However, I don't think you are." I was not too weak to add that.

Just then there flashed across my mind the recollection of a dream I had the night before, the same night the Christians were praying for me. I decided to relate it to Dr. Jarman, since it was brief and seemed to support his contention that my desire to die was encouraged by malevolent forces.

"I preface my account of this dream," I told him, "by saying that I know it did not come from God. It had a Satanic source, of that I am certain. But this was the dream:

"It was night, and there was a storm outside. I was alone in the house when a door opened, and my mother (who died eleven years ago) came in. She was dressed in a long nightgown. She was old and frail, sick and trembling.

" 'I'm frightened,' she said, clutching my arm. 'Come and stay with me.'

"I agreed to go with her, and we went into another room, the room where she had been sleeping. I started to get into bed in this other room when the dream ended.

"Now it is quite evident," I said to Dr. Jarman, "that this was not from God. The dream was shrouded in the darkness of night, for one thing. It is not night where my mother is. There is no night there. Neither is there old age, illness, or fear. But she is in 'another room,' so to speak. And I am perfectly willing to go there."

Dr. Jarman voiced the opinion that the dream was an additional work of Satan to foster my wish to die. His definite assertion was: "God has something more for you to do, Carmen. And the devil wants to stop you from doing it."

"If that is the case," I answered, "he has been accomplishing his purpose. Physically, emotionally, financially, I am a beaten, worn-down, broken and defeated person."

"You are not going to stay that way," he said. "God is going to take all that the devil has done to you, and all the destruction you have done to yourself by wrong reactions, unhealthy thoughts and feelings, and He is going to turn them into good. You are going to write another book, and it is going to be a real blessing to many people."

"I don't see how that could be possible," I sighed.

But strangely enough, about that time I began to notice something stirring within me. Something I would have called, in my less negative days—hope.

"A funny thing is happening to me, Dr. Jarman," I commented. "I feel a little better. And by the way, I do appreciate those kind Christians in Arlington, Virginia, who don't even know me, but who were concerned enough to undergird me in prayer. Please thank them for me. And thank you for all that you are always doing to help me."

Before the conversation concluded, he again referred to the book. My reply was, "Well, if God is in it, He will confirm it. He always has in the past."

Much to my astonishment, He did that very thing!

The first confirmation was not long in coming. It was part of the second phone call of the morning, this one from my doctor.

"You sound brighter today," he observed.

When I told him about Dr. Jarman's long-distance call and his revelation regarding a new book, the doctor immediately replied, "I have always known that you were going to write another book."

This took me aback, for I had repeatedly informed him, as well as others, that I had no intention of ever writing again. "Life has made that impossible," was the way I put it; and that was an absolute certainty as far as I was concerned.

Now, here was the doctor flatly affirming his conviction that the very opposite was true! I could only repeat my remark that at least suffering was one subject I had considerable knowledge and experience of, as he and I both well knew. That very week I had come to him with a different and painful complaint, asking, "Where can I go to get a new body?"

He had smiled, but had admitted that I could use one. "You do seem to have no let-up when it comes to ailment after ailment," he noted, "one on top of another—plus injuries from accidents, and surgery thrown in for good measure."

My telephone conversation with the doctor ended, and I began to reflect on what both he and Dr. Jarman had said. "They were probably just trying to cheer me up," I decided, "to give me something to look forward to in an attempt to bring me out of my apathy and depression."

Yet oddly enough, my spirits were indeed lifted . . . Was it possible they could be right? I felt a sudden quickening in my mind, and an inexplicable lightness in my soul.

"Oh God," I cried out, "do You really have a plan and a purpose behind all of this? To write a book about suffering—is that Your will for me?"

After a moment or two of silence, I began to pray.

"Lord, I could not undertake this on the strength of man's words alone. I have lived too long to put my trust in anything man says. I have a hard enough time trusting You, dear God—Of course," I hastened to add, "that isn't Your fault. It is mine, and I ask Your forgiveness for this, as well as for all my other faults and failings."

Again there was silence for a while. Finally I said, "Lord, if it truly is Your will, I will do it. But I must have Your personal confirmation. I trust You to give it to me in Your own way and at Your own time."

I pondered the matter a little longer, then finished my prayer by telling the Lord, "Maybe I'll get a pencil and a notebook and see what happens. I haven't anything to lose. If the well is dry, I will soon know it."

Now, I don't recommend this as a model prayer for aspiring writers, or for anyone else. But I do recommend plain honesty in talking to God, and in asking Him for verification and for His guidance before rushing into anything on our own.

With that same plain honesty, I will relate what occurred following the prayer.

As God is my witness, my mind was instantly inundated by some kind of spiritual flood. "I think we hit a gusher!" was my irreverent exclamation.

First came the title, *What About Us Who Are Not Healed?* Then came the opening words, and subsequently a flow of them—paragraph after paragraph. Then a voice sounded in my consciousness:

"Just tell it as it is," spoke the unseen Personage.

With a surge of delight, I recognized the source of that voice. It was the glorious and wonderful presence of my dear Companion of old, the blessed Holy Spirit. He had been with me in such sweet intimacy all the while we wrote my first books. My heavenly Helper, my Teacher, whose voice, though inaudible to human ears, is clear as crystal to spiritual ears that are open to Him.

There is no mistaking that precious presence, just as there is no mistaking His absence. And I am acquainted with both.

Now, I do not mean to imply that heretofore I had been bereft of the Holy Spirit, for He is with every true Christian from the time of conversion. Jesus promised an indwelling of the Spirit that is abiding and constant. He also promised the experience of being baptized in the Holy Ghost, an added enduement of power for service. This has been my privilege and joy for a number of years.

Beyond both of these, there is still another manifestation of the Spirit's presence that comes upon me occasionally. I would call it an anointing. It is always temporary, for a specific purpose—usually that of speaking before a group of people. Not that I am a speaker, but when I am asked to speak, an anointing sometimes comes. If it didn't, the people who had to listen to me would get nothing from the Lord.

But this inrush of His Spirit for the purpose of writing a book is over and above all these other things.

The only way I can describe it is to say the Spirit fills me in a greater degree or measure than I have known before. He quickens me—even my mortal body, so that I do not need the normal sleep or food that I regularly require. But He does not heal me.

When this quickening first happened several years ago, I fully anticipated that bodily healing would accompany it. But I remained physically as I was. We simply transcended those physical conditions, and went on with our work.

This spiritual influx also illumines my mind. He does not make me the fountain of all wisdom, nor does He make me a great writer. But He does take what I am and what I offer Him— for I give Him my nothing in its totality. He maximizes it and uses it to edify the body of Christ, and I am included in that edification. My soul is expanded, my spirit elevated. He communes with me in a fellowship unexcelled by any in this world.

Surely this is love divine bestowed on a most unworthy vessel!

One might expect that all of this would work such transformation that my family and friends would scarcely recognize me. There is marked improvement—and God knows I need it—

As I write these very words, I realize that I have finally put the truth in a nutshell. "God knows I need it," and that is why He comes in this unique and blissful way.

David put it in another nutshell: "This is the LORD's doing; it is marvelous in our eyes" (Ps. 118:23).

Here then was the personal part of the confirmation for which I had prayed. God was providing the necessary equipment to accomplish a particular task, in order that I might fulfill His purpose for me.

"So be it, Lord," I said aloud. "You know where You are leading, even if I don't. Whatever You have to impart is of much value—*that*, I definitely know. With Your help, I shall try to pass it on."

I couldn't keep from adding, "But in the process, I would appreciate a little relief from all this pain—if You don't mind."

II

"Thou Didst Lay Affliction on Our Loins"

(Ps. 66:11 RSV)

I said, "My leg is killing me. I can hardly walk!"
The doctor said, "You have severe muscle strain and
    inflammation. Walk as little as possible."
God said, "I will walk in them; and I will be their God,
    and they shall be my people" (II Cor. 6:16).

It is now the next day. How nice it would be if I could say,
"No sooner had I commenced the book than all pain left me! I
was able to discontinue the diet I had been on for days—warm
half-and-half, augmented only by a little cream of wheat, potato
soup, and a poached egg without salt or pepper."

I would like to tell you that I put away the heating pad, that
energy filled my body, that all obstacles miraculously disap-
peared, and I was supernaturally made every whit whole.

Yes, that would be wonderful to say, and even more wonderful to experience. The only trouble is, it would not be true.
Things just didn't happen that way. Actually, I was stricken by
new pain—worse than what I already had elsewhere—this time

in my left leg. I found I could hardly walk.

"Oh no!" I exclaimed upon discovering that my infirmities were not decreased in the slightest, but rather increased. "This is adding insult to injury, Lord," I protested. "No wonder this book is about suffering. The way things are going so far, I'm not going to be able to suffer through it. Lord, I cannot understand why You don't intervene in my behalf."

Do you know what His answer to this was? Certainly it was not what I would have liked to have heard. My idea of a fitting response would have been something like this:

"Carmen, you poor little child of Mine. I have heard your cry, I have seen your affliction, your oppression, and your willingness to serve Me. I will gather you in My arms, comfort you, touch your body, and restore you to health. You will live out your days in peace, prosperity, and happiness."

Sorry to report, that is not what He said. These were His exact words:

"O death, where is thy sting? O grave, where is thy victory?"

In spite of myself, I had to laugh. "What on earth do You mean by quoting that particular Scripture to me, Lord?" I asked in amazement.

"You have been wanting to die," He said, "asking Me to take you home because I do not heal you or answer all your other prayers in the way you think they should be answered."

"Yes, but that's not the answer," I objected.

"That is the answer you thought would solve all your problems."

I got the point. "All right, Lord. I accept correction in that regard. Since we started the book, I've stopped wanting to die. I want to live. I want to glorify You in my body, soul, and spirit. I see that the death-wish is really the coward's way out of an unpleasant situation— But Lord, You know I always have been a coward."

"I know," He said, but He said it tenderly. Then He declared firmly, "Be strong, and of a good courage."

"Moses spoke those words to Joshua," I broke in. "In fact, the Lord repeated them to Joshua three times after that."

12

"I shall probably have to repeat them even more times to you," was His quiet rejoinder.

Properly subdued, I asked Him to pardon the interruption, and to continue what He had to say about death's sting and the grave's victory. "Your student is ready to listen," I told Him.

He began by instructing me to look up the Scripture. "See what is written just before those words."

I usually have my Bible close at hand. Turning quickly to I Corinthians 15, I read aloud the preceding verse, verse 54:

"So when this corruptible shall have put on incorruption, and this mortal shall have put on immortality, then shall be brought to pass the saying that is written, Death is swallowed up in victory."

"Where is that saying written?" I asked. A glance at the margin told me it was from Isaiah 25:8.

"Isaiah!" I exclaimed. "I might have known it!"

You see, Isaiah is the book in the Bible the Lord has used most often to speak personally to me. It has become exceedingly dear because of that reason. The first Scripture He ever applied to me was from Isaiah. It was this: "Fear not, for I have redeemed you; I have called you by name, you are mine" (Isa. 43:1 RSV). This happened soon after my new-birth experience, in which the Lord Jesus Christ had called me by name. Later I began wondering whether He really had done such a thing. Perhaps I only imagined it. Yet it had seemed so real. It was then that the Holy Spirit led me to that particular passage and personalized it in an unmistakable way. I remember I fell on my knees with gratitude, thrilled at receiving positive written assurance that He truly did call me by name when He redeemed me.

And such as I am, I have been His ever since.

In the years that have ensued, His customary way of answering or confirming something I have very much wanted to know has been through His Word. His Word is still the final authority as far as I am concerned. It is the only authority, when all is said and done.

I lost no time in flipping the pages of my Bible back to Isaiah

25:8. With a heart brimful with joy, I prepared to savor each word.

And here it was:

"He will swallow up death in victory; and the Lord GOD will wipe away tears from off all faces; and the rebuke of his people shall he take away from off all the earth; for the LORD hath spoken it."

The Holy Spirit's teaching on suffering had begun, and this was the divinely selected answer to the question, *What About Us Who Are Not Healed?* I knew that it was meant individually for me, and collectively for all who suffer in body, mind, emotions, spirit, or any of life's affairs. It gives blanket coverage, and surpasses any insurance policy—health or life.

I tell you the truth—if my leg had not hurt so badly, I would have jumped out of bed and again fallen on my knees in loving appreciation to the Lord for beginning to teach me once more in the old familiar way! But unfortunately, I was in no shape to do it.

Someone may be wondering how a single verse of Scripture could cause such an overwhelming reaction. It was because so much meaning was conveyed along with it!

Here is my attempt to put into words what that verse said to me:

All that is of death will be consumed by the Lord. No matter what the world, the flesh, and the devil can, have, and will continue to throw at me—and at any of God's people—Satan is a defeated foe. Suffering ends in victory, and victory begins now! Victory is mine, victory is yours; victory in Jesus. Hallelujah!

Whether or not the pain, the weakness, and the suffering are removed from us here on earth is not the vital issue. The important thing is this: Nothing that has to do with death—that includes sickness, old age, and cessation of human life—can defeat us. Christ has taken out death's sting. The grave has no victory. Not for me, or for any of God's people.

The verse also assured me that in God's own time, He will remove all suffering of whatever kind it is that causes such pain, sorrow, limitation, and difficulty. He will do this for each

14

person on the face of the earth who belongs to Him.

Simultaneously with the message came the awareness that in God's own way, He was giving the very answer I had wished for in the first place—the answer I thought He ought to have given when I complained about my suffering. He does have compassion on His child, He hears the cry, He sees the distress and the injustices that are done. He knows the heart that is turned to Him. He will gather in His arms, wipe the tears from the eyes, and give loving comfort.

Furthermore, the verse had a floodlight shining on His promise to take away the "rebuke"—reproach, shame, and defeat—all the exterior negative experiences in life, as well as the discreditable interior character traits. For as Christians, we sometimes are a disgrace to His name. At least I am.

Yet here was God Himself promising the peace, prosperity, and happiness that I had hoped for—not just temporal, but eternal—everlasting, forevermore. Yes, all that is of evil will be "swallowed up" in triumphant victory. For the Lord hath spoken it. To me personally.

What a God! What a Savior!

Next I looked up the Old Testament Scripture from which Paul in I Corinthians 15:55 quoted the words, "O death, where is thy sting? O grave, where is thy victory?" Hosea 13:14.

When I turned to Hosea 13, my eyes first fell on verse 9. It said:

"O Carmen, thou hast destroyed thyself; but in me is thine help."

(I know it uses the name "Israel" instead of "Carmen." But in the application, "Israel" meant me. The Lord has often called me "Jacob" or "Israel"—even "Jerusalem" on one occasion.)

In that verse, He underlined the lesson that my death-wish was self-destroying, but in Him is deliverance—especially from myself.

The exact reference verse, the 14th, stated: "I will ransom them from the power of the grave; I will redeem them from death; O death, I will be thy plagues; O grave, I will be thy

15

destruction; repentance shall be hid from mine eyes."

As I finished reading it aloud, my Teacher said to me, "When I first quoted the words 'O death, where is thy sting? O grave, where is thy victory?' did you know there was a divine promise concealed within them?"

"I certainly didn't," I replied.

"What is that promise?" He asked.

"The promise is that God will pay the price to deliver His own from death and the grave. He will destroy the powers of hell, and He will not relent in His purpose."

Then it struck me—

"Christ is the promise hidden in that Scripture!" I exclaimed. "It was fulfilled when Jesus gave His life a ransom for many. I said I couldn't understand why You did not intervene in my behalf. But You already have! You still are intervening! Christ is my victory, the One who intercedes for me. This Scripture guarantees me triumph over everything, even death itself."

"You have a goodly heritage, Carmen," He declared.

"For which I thank You, Lord," I told Him most fervently. "Thank You for my blessed Redeemer, and for the future when all those glorious promises in Isaiah 25:8 will be completely fulfilled. But about the present—"

I halfway hesitated, then went ahead with the sentence. "Couldn't I have just a little less then, and a little more now? I need it worse now than I will then."

"What do you need now?"

"I need healing, for one thing. This leg is killing me. The pain is right in the hollow of my thigh. It feels as out-of-joint as Jacob's was after his all-night wrestling match with the angel. Won't You please do something about that?"

I really did not expect an answer to this latest plea in my long record of pleading for physical relief. But to my surprise, in a moment or two I heard Him say, "If you will be as Jacob, and not let Me go until I bless you, then you too will prevail."

That is all He said. He withdrew His presence, and I was left alone.

Dragging my shrunken sinew out of bed, I limped my painful

way to the grocery store which my husband and I own and operate. Or rather, it owns and operates us, for we have to be there long hours of every day—whether we are sick or well, dead or alive. How can I get well, how can I prevail in a situation like that?

I guess the only possible way is just as He said—"By not letting Me go until I bless you."

But why does everything have to be the hard way for me, Lord? Why can't I have it soft and easy like other wives? And anyway, I'm no wrestler!

III

"And Had Suffered Many Things of Many Physicians"

(Mark 5:26)

The various doctors said, "You have sinusitis, labyrin-
   thitis, tonsillitis, bronchitis, neuritis, arthritis, gastri-
   tis, colitis, cystitis, and sciatica."
I said, "I've got them bad. Why?"
The Holy Spirit said, "Why not?"

"Good morning, dear Lord . . .

"We might as well start out that way, because it seems that's
the way this book is going. You and I talking about suffering.
I'm doing the suffering, and You're doing the talking."

"I get a word in now and then," He said, "when I have the
chance."

Somewhat abashed, I replied, "Well, I hope You will give me
an answer to the 'why' of suffering—at least of mine. I know
there are millions of other sufferers, many whose condition is so
much worse I am ashamed to mention my own in comparison.
But there are also millions who have very little, if any, real suffering all their lives. Why is there such inequity regarding this,
Lord?

18

"Before You say anything," I went on, "I also hope You will not give me the same complex answer involving Creation that God gave poor Job. Remember I'm not like his four friends, trying to put the blame here, there, and everywhere—especially on Job—and each of them acting as though he were a great oracle of wisdom, even to expounding on the government of God."

I continued with my own expounding by adding, "I'm not even like Job, who was righteous in his own eyes. I know I am not righteous. And as for appointing myself an authority on anything—that I am not either. So it wouldn't help to say to me, 'Who is this that darkeneth counsel by words without knowledge?'

"I know I do not have any real knowledge. That is what I am looking to You for. By the way, Lord, why didn't God tell Job straight out that Satan was the one to blame for all his troubles? . . . All right, I'll be quiet now, Lord. I will just sit here in bed, ice bag on my leg, heating pad on my chest, and let these horrible-tasting charcoal tablets the doctor prescribed dissolve in my mouth while You speak to me."

It was a few silent, empty, blank moments before I heard His reply.

"Did you say I was doing the talking?" the Spirit inquired. "In regard to suffering, you wanted an answer to your question, 'Why?' Let Me ask you, 'Why not?' "

"Lord, You do give the strangest answers!"

Then the Holy Spirit began to teach. "In the last words that Jesus spoke to His disciples, He told them that in the world they would have tribulation. This was just before Gethsemane, and what you call His 'high-priestly prayer.' You looked up that word 'tribulation.' You found that it meant 'distress, pressure, affliction, anguish, burdens, and trouble.' "

"Yes, I did, Lord," I interrupted, "and I remember I said that was one promise I have realized to the fullest."

"Have you suffered to the point of shedding your life's blood?"

"No," I admitted.

He continued. "If the disciples suffered what they did, and if more recent saints, such as those you particularly esteem—Fanny Crosby, blind from early infancy; St. Teresa of Avila; Christina Rossetti; Martha Snell Nicholson—suffered almost constantly all their lives, do you think you are better than they, that you should expect to escape suffering?"

"Oh no, Lord!" I hastened to assert. "You know I'm not worthy to be considered in the same category with them."

"And if Jesus Himself in the days of His flesh suffered beyond all of these, should you wonder why you are called upon to bear your share of pain and trial?"

To this, I couldn't help responding with the same complaint I have so often voiced. "But I get more than my share, Lord! I seldom ever know a day without pain—pain of more than one kind—often two or three kinds at the same time. And this has been going on for years! You know that's true, Lord."

"Shall we look at the record," He replied, "since you bring it up? Paint the picture as you see it."

"Well, I was born half-dead. They couldn't get me to start breathing. I must have had a premonition of what I was getting into and preferred to stay where I was. Then my father poured whiskey, of all things, into me as a stimulant. No wonder I've had stomach trouble ever since! Probably burnt out the lining right off the bat. Before my mother was able to care for me, my grandmother fed me raw apples—raw apples, mind you—scraped, I assume. This almost finished me off."

"Yet you managed to survive," the Holy Spirit remarked calmly. "Just as your brother Dean survived, despite the little pieces of glass you fed him while playing doctor."

"But I was only a child, Lord! I didn't know what I was doing."

"Neither did they. So quit blaming others, and resume your story."

Squelched again, but only momentarily, I continued. "I suppose You would consider it blaming others if I pointed out the fact that I inherited a weak, frail body. Besides that, the doctor said that much of my trouble is the result of a structural condition I was born with. Why wasn't I fortunate enough to be like the many who come into this world strong and healthy, and who stay that way almost all their days?"

"You were fortunate enough not to enter this world crippled, blind, deaf, or mentally retarded. How thankful are you for this?" admonished the Spirit. "Granted that there are things over which you had no control, let us take a look at some of the things for which you yourself have been responsible."

"You mean the damage I've done to my body by so many years of hard work?" I queried.

"Much of what you term 'hard work' was unnecessary labor you placed upon yourself by your own choice."

"Lord, how can You say that? You know it certainly was not my choice to buy a grocery store and put me in it every day and night for years on end, besides keeping up a home and breaking my back—which constantly aches with arthritis—doing yard work that my husband ought to do."

"Who chose him for your husband?"

"I did."

"Would you say that he made the ideal choice in you?"

"No, I wouldn't. But how much judgment does a seventeen-year-old girl have? Especially when a young man seems so much in love with her, treats her like a princess on a throne, and promises to take her out of an unhappy home situation. He was a good church person, on top of that. Are marriages supposed to be made in heaven?"

Now, perhaps I should apologize to those who may feel that the Holy Spirit does not engage in the kind of "earthy" banter I am recounting. Some may find it difficult to believe He has a sense of humor at all, or that a member of the Godhead would condescend to spend so much time talking with a human being, particularly a woman.

If I am offending anyone in this matter, please forgive me. I have found that the Lord does have a sense of humor, along with all His other perfect attributes.

And as for condescension, how much lower could a member

of the Godhead condescend than to make Himself of no reputation, take upon Himself the form of a servant, being made in the likeness of men; and be spat upon, slapped, mocked, reviled, beaten with stripes, nailed to a cross, and die as a sacrificial offering to redeem a world of lost sinners?

"The Holy Spirit doesn't talk to *me* like that," someone may be saying.

I would answer by asking, "How much time do you spend talking to Him? And more important, how much time do you spend studying, meditating upon, and hiding in your heart all that He already has said in His sacred Word?"

It is not my intention to give the impression that we can construe everything that pops into our head as coming from the Lord. Definitely not. But during my years of earnest, avid Bible study, and my looking to the Lord in prayer for answers to questions that are of spiritual importance, I have found that He does not refuse to speak to me. How could we have fellowship if He never talked to me?

It is my firm conviction that if we are fulfilling His will and purpose for our lives, He is right there alongside of us to teach, to bring to our remembrance, to guide us into truth, to reveal Christ, and to abide with us and in us forever. Just as Jesus said He would.

"Sorry, Lord, for the digression. Shall we get back to the subject at hand? What were You talking about? Oh yes, me and my suffering . . . "

IV
"Is There No Balm in Gilead?"

(Jer. 8:22)

I said, "Satan is to blame, my parents are to blame, my husband is to blame, life is to blame."
The Spirit said, "Blame yourself for a few things."
The Bible said sin is to blame. "By one man's disobedience, many were made sinners. . . . Sin came into the world through one man, and death through sin; and so death spread to all men, because all men sinned" (Rom. 5:19,12 RSV).

"Suppose we summarize the principal things you have learned so far," my heavenly Teacher said, "in order to keep them clearly in mind and help you understand where we're going."

"All right," I replied. "First, I saw how wrong and self-destructive has been my wish to die. There would be no victory in death or in the grave. My death-wish was just an open invitation for Satan to buffet me with blow after blow in body and mind. You caused me to recognize that as a gross error on my part; and with Your help, I have renounced it for good.

"You also made me aware that death, like everything else, is in Your hands. When Jesus gave His life for us, He removed death's sting and robbed the grave of any victory for those who are in Him. He is the promise concealed in those very words. In Christ, God has provided all that is necessary for us to triumph over any experience of life. And He is even now interceding in our behalf.

"Furthermore," I continued, "God promised to remove all sorrow and shame from my life when my redemption is complete, when this physical body has been changed—or raised—to immortality. I even remember the relevant Scriptures—I Corinthians 15:54, Isaiah 25:8, and Hosea 13:14."

"Good," said the Spirit. "That was lesson one. Now what came after that?"

"Well, I guess you could say we took up the subject of where to put the blame for suffering."

"On that subject you were most vocal," He commented.

"I did admit my own mistakes though, Lord."

"Some of them."

"We don't have to go into all of them, do we, Lord?" I asked with a tinge of horror.

"No. Just the ones that you share in common with many other people and with a number of sufferers who will identify with you."

"We who suffer . . . " I sighed. "Our name is legion, is it not, Lord?"

His answer had a depth of compassion in it. "You are indeed many."

"I know that is not Your doing, Lord. It is the work of Satan, and of man himself. Part of the curse, You might say, that came into existence with the entrance of sin into the world. But what can we do about it? We don't know what goes on behind the scenes of our lives, any more than Job knew who really was to blame for all his misery. He even thought You were to blame, Lord."

"Have you ever had such a thought, Carmen?" He asked.

"Lord, You know all things. I have not so much blamed You for my sufferings as I have been disappointed in You for not

24

doing more about them. I don't understand why You allow so much physical suffering to come my way. You help me in countless other aspects of life, answering my prayers bountifully. But when it comes to relief from bodily affliction—even the limiting of it, or just occasional respite—Your ears seem deaf to my pleas, as well as to the pleas of others in my behalf. Why is this, dear Lord?"

He gave this answer:

"My ears are not deaf to the cries of My children, nor is My arm powerless to deliver. Because I do not answer as you desire does not mean I am unmindful or unheeding. My ways are not your ways, and My timing is not regulated according to the will of man."

"I know that ultimately You will heal me of everything, Lord. Does that mean that for now it is Your will not to heal me?"

"That is not what I said," was His instant reproof.

"Some men teach that it is always Your will to heal. That it is Your will to heal all believers of all things at all times."

"Men teach many things," was His noncommittal reply.

"They support their teachings with Scripture, Lord."

He was quick to correct me. "They *use* Scripture to support their teachings. There can be a difference between what they deduce from the Scripture and what the Scripture says."

"In other words," said I, "their deductions are not always the truth, the whole truth, and nothing but the truth."

He made no response to this sage observation, so I continued. "They quote Matthew 8:16 where it says that Jesus 'healed all that were sick, that it might be fulfilled which was spoken by Isaiah the prophet, saying, He himself took our infirmities, and bore our sicknesses' (SCO). They add what Peter said: 'By whose stripes ye were healed' (I Pet. 2:24). They throw in the third verse of the 103rd Psalm about the Lord 'who healeth all thy diseases.' "

"Do these teachers themselves always manifest immediate, infallible, and complete healing?" asked the Spirit.

I had to smile. "Not any that I have met."

"When they pray for people, are all the sick healed?"

25

"No, not all of them. But healings do occur. I have heard many testimonies of those who have been healed solely through spiritual means. I myself have witnessed and known several individuals who received miraculous healings. Most of these happened in large meetings."

"Did all who came for healing receive healing?" He further questioned.

"No, they did not."

"Then on the basis of what you have witnessed in the lives of hundreds of Christians, as well as in the lives of those who teach that it is always God's will to heal, I gather that you do not agree with their teaching."

"Lord, You know that I don't. I just wanted to find out if You did. By the way, what do You say about a Christian going to a doctor?"

"I am not against physicians," He replied. "I have one on My staff. His name is Luke."

"To return to the summation of our lesson material," said the Holy Spirit, "you recalled our talk about where to put the blame for suffering. Are you forgetting the interchange we had over your thinking you should be exempt from suffering? At least from so much of it. Do you remember your many questions 'Why?' "

"I remember Your answer, 'Why not?' " I told Him. "I'm still wounded from that."

"Let me ask you this," He said. "Do you think suffering can teach anything? If so, what have you learned from it?"

I thought for a moment. "I would say that it can teach compassion for others, endurance in trial, patient acceptance of things over which we have no control. To be honest, I would have to add that it can also educate one in weariness, bitterness, resentment, perplexity, and despondency. I certainly learned those things from it."

"What did Jesus learn from the things which He suffered?"

I knew the scriptural answer to that one. "He learned obedience, Hebrews 5:8," was my prompt reply.

"Then permit me to ask you another question," my Teacher stated. "If Jesus—the very Son of God—by the experience of suffering learned something that was needful for Him, do you think that you have no need of learning by suffering? Is the servant greater than her Master?"

"Oh no, Lord!" I protested. "I know that I need to learn a lot more than obedience."

"But you would like to learn it an easier way, is that it?" was His mild prod.

"Yes," I answered lamely, "I guess that's it. Isn't there some other way, Lord?"

As soon as I asked the question, it sounded as stupid to me as it must have sounded to the Spirit. Sure enough, He did not dignify it with a reply, but instead instructed me to turn to Hebrews 5:8-10 and also to Hebrews 2:10, and take a good long look at both of those passages.

I decided to examine them in a couple of other translations besides the King James, with which I was most familiar. (Sometimes we are too familiar with a passage. We are so accustomed to its wording that it becomes just that to us—words—and the impact and depth of its meaning escapes us.)

The Amplified version brought out that it was "active, special" obedience Jesus learned through what He suffered. "His completed experience" made Him perfect "in equipment" to become the Author and Source of eternal salvation to all those who obey Him.

"In other words," I said aloud to the Lord, "if Jesus was going to teach and expect us to obey Him, He had to learn obedience Himself by obeying the Father. Though He was God manifest in flesh, He still needed the experience of suffering in order to complete His mission of becoming our Savior and High Priest."

I found that the Living Bible said the same thing:

"Even though Jesus was God's Son, he had to learn from experience what it was like to obey, when obeying meant suffering. It was after he had proved himself perfect in this experience that Jesus became the Giver of eternal salvation to all those who obey him. For remember that God has chosen him to be a High

Priest" (Heb. 5:8-10).

"We prove ourselves through suffering then, don't we, Lord?" I asked. "Or rather, suffering proves us, tests us. Hopefully, it purifies us, burns out a lot of dross. This is needful if we are to be perfected—grow up, become mature sons of God instead of remaining babes in Christ."

"That is correct," He said, then added, "There are many Christians who never grow up. They are content to remain babies and little children. True, they do escape the suffering and painful experiences that are a part of spiritual maturity. But did you ever know a mature Christian who had suffered little or nothing? He who suffers little, matures little."

"I must be aging fast then, Lord."

I turned then to the other passage in Hebrews (2:10) about "the captain of our salvation being made perfect through suffering." This is the way the Amplified put it:

"For it was an act worthy of God and fitting to the divine nature that He . . . in bringing many sons into glory, should make the Pioneer of their salvation perfect (that is, should bring to maturity the human experience necessary for a perfect equipment for His office as High Priest) through suffering."

"That expression 'making Jesus perfect' confuses a lot of people, Lord," I said. "We know He was not imperfect previously. He was perfect before He did any suffering, for He was without sin of any kind. He was Deity. The word 'perfect' could not mean that He had to be made 'flawless.' "

"Why don't you look up its precise meaning in your Greek dictionary?" suggested the Spirit.

When I did, I found that the scope of the word "perfect" meant "to complete, accomplish, consummate in character, consecrate, finish, fulfill."

"Succinctly put, then," I stated to my Teacher, "Jesus could not have brought to a complete end, or have totally fulfilled the work He came to do, without suffering. That was the way He attained His goal."

"Carmen," He answered, "you may have difficulty digesting earthly food, but your spiritual digestion functions fairly well."

"And I don't have to subsist on milk in that realm, do I, Lord?"

"No," He agreed. "You belong with those who can handle the meat of the Word—as far as digesting it is concerned."

"But when it comes to assimilating it—appropriating it into the substance of my life—" my words began to falter, "I don't do too well; is that it?"

Returning to the Scripture, I was thrilled with the Living Bible's wording of Hebrews 2:10:

"It was right and proper that God, who made everything for his own glory, should allow Jesus to suffer, for in doing this he was bringing vast multitudes of God's people to heaven; for his suffering made Jesus a perfect Leader, one fit to bring them into their salvation."

"Lord," I told Him, "now I understand a little better why You have allowed me to suffer so much. I am not one to be satisfied with infantile or juvenile things—even spiritual ones. My aspirations go much higher than that. But 'high things' have a high price, too. And when that price is suffering, I have not been too willing to pay the cost, have I?"

"I would say the spirit is willing," was my Teacher's response, "but the flesh is weak."

"Lord, strengthen me, help me, uphold me!" I implored.

"Isn't that what I promised to do?" He asked; and I knew whereof He spoke—Isaiah 41:10, of course.

"Forgive me, Lord," I begged, "for complaining so much, and for being disappointed in You for not removing my suffering from me."

V

"The Tongue of the Wise Is Health"

(Prov. 12:18)

The Christian customer said, "I fear many things. The
   thing I fear most . . . "
The Christian Carmen said, "I fear many things too."
The Bible said, "Fear not." It said it many times, from
   Genesis to Revelation.

Today is a holiday. Memorial Day—the day of remembrance.
"Lord, I am remembering some happenings and some conver-
sations that occurred during the last two days since You and I
met to work on our book together. Could we talk about them?
They have a direct bearing on our subject."
"Go ahead," He told me.
I knew that He had been present as well as I when these
incidents took place, but if I didn't bring them up for discussion,
I would not get His reaction to them. I began to relate the first
conversation.
Saturday afternoon in the store, Jacobina (that's what I sometimes call myself when the Lord and I are talking; the name is

30

especially appropriate since I have this leg injury) came limping down the aisle with the cash-register drawers balanced on her twisted hip, and encounter a customer pushing her shopping cart. Both my husband and I consider this particular customer to be one of the most beautiful women who comes in our market.

"Good afternoon, Fashion-plate," I greeted her, for she always looks so lovely—every hair in place, her face exquisitely made up, her figure trim and attractively dressed.

"What's the matter with you?" she inquired, noticing the halting leg.

"Not a thing!" I exclaimed with a lively note of joy in my voice. "I'm on top of the world spiritually, though near the bottom of the heap physically."

"How can that be?" she demanded skeptically.

I hesitated for a moment before giving her my answer.

She and I frequently chat together. Almost every occasion turns out to be an inventory of our mutual aches and pains. The whole wretched mess of them. We both look pretty good on the outside—she definitely does—but what is on the inside is another matter. This we usually dredge up for detailed dissertation with each other. People see the "retail" side of us. We take inventory "wholesale"—what our bodies actually cost us in the way of misery and doctor bills.

This time, however, I decided not to go into that.

"I couldn't anyway, Lord," I explained to him, deviating briefly from my story. "I was too happy, in spite of my pains. You see, working with You on our book, and having Your blessed presence so close and companiable with me again—the way I had it when we wrote our first books several years ago—has exhilarated me, lifted me above my self."

I told the customer that I was filled with joy because I had begun a new book. "It's about suffering," I said.

"You're full of joy writing about suffering?" she asked, incredulous at the very thought.

"Yes," I replied. "It's the strangest thing I've ever experienced."

"I heard a sermon on suffering last Sunday," she remarked.

"Our minister spoke glowingly of all that suffering does to refine the character. He said it makes the heart more tender and compassionate. He preached a lot of inspiring things about suffering. The only thing lacking was that he doesn't do much suffering himself."

"Not like you and I do!" was my instant judgment.

This was typical of me, not knowing the man or a thing about him. I then launched into a sermon of my own on how suffering must serve some purpose for good, else God would not allow so much of it to so many. When I got to the part about suffering being the chief cause of my death-wish, she interrupted me.

"I haven't ever wished to die," she confided. "But there is one thing that scares me to death about dying." (The humor of her choice of words just now strikes me.) "It isn't that I am afraid I won't go to heaven. Our church teaches that once we have been saved, our salvation is eternally assured. But I am terribly afraid that I will lose my mind while I'm in the process of dying— maybe from all the suffering—and blaspheme God."

"Blaspheme God!" I exclaimed aghast.

"Yes," she confessed. "I am afraid I'll say to my children or grandchildren, 'There isn't any God. Don't you get hooked on religion the way I have been all my life.' Naturally, I would never say that in my right mind. But suffering, and the drugs they give you when you're dying, can cause you to say a lot of weird things. Of course," she finished, "I would be out of my mind."

"You would have to be," I commented bluntly.

"Another thing worries me," she went on. "I hear women say, 'I get up in the morning and I feel terrific. Bursting with energy all day.' " Then, pointing to herself, she said, "Yet here I am—tired before the day starts. When I get out of bed in the morning, I say, 'I wonder what's going to hurt today?' "

Jacobina replied, "Well, if I *can* get out of bed in the morning, I say, 'I wonder what *isn't* going to hurt!' "

We laughed, and then she asked me, "Seriously, what is the answer? Is God partial? Some women seem to feel good all the time. Do you think they really do?"

"I doubt it," said Thomasina.

"Well, be that as it may," observed the customer, "I know that I bring a lot of trouble on myself by doing too much. Especially for my family."

"I do that too," I said. "You know, you and I are easy targets for the undermining of our bodies by both Satan and ourselves. We're middle-aged, nervous, anxious perfectionists who have always worked too hard by choice, or by being forced to. What do you suppose we would do if God were to heal us of all our suffering—of everything that ails us?"

She did not waver for a split second. "I would probably go out and raise Cain having a good time, living it up!" she announced boldly.

Somewhat shaken by this unexpected reply, I mumbled, "I don't know what I would do. I think I would be so surprised to find my body free from all physical affliction that I would be convinced I must be mentally ill."

"Now, what do You think about all this conversation, Lord?" I asked, when I had come to the end of my lengthy narrative.

There was a pause, then the Holy Spirit gave this answer: "It reminds me of a line from William Shakespeare—'Much Ado About Nothing.' "

"Lord!" I protested. "Why did You let me go ahead and write all of this?"

"Because," He replied, "it well illustrates how much time and energy is wasted by too many people on inconsequentials, and how much importance is attached to trivialities and foolish fears." He went on to say, "However, there are those who will identify with it, to their profit. As they did last night."

"Oh yes," I answered, recalling our Sunday evening service at church . . .

It had been an unusual service, one so delightful that no one wanted to go home when nine o'clock came. It was well past ten before the meeting terminated, and we sang, "Blest be the tie that binds our hearts in Christian love . . . "

The service did not begin in a delightful spirit. It began in the doldrums. The holiday weekend had so depleted the small congregation that only a faithful few were there. In vain, the song leader labored to lift the atmosphere. Even the pastor appeared downcast.

When it came time for prayer requests, one of the young men rose to his feet and spoke about the spirit of discouragement that seemed to be prevailing over the elders of the church. I knew this was my cue, for my spirit was full of rejoicing.

I got up to speak. We are free to do this at any time in our services, particularly the Sunday evening service. And I knew it was what the Lord wanted me to do.

"For once you were obedient to the Spirit's prompting," the Teacher's voice interrupted my reminiscence.

"Yes, Lord," I answered, "and I am glad I was."

I told the congregation how I had permitted the devil to discourage me, and that my prolonged physical suffering, combined with business worries and other trials, had caused me to want to die.

"For a long time I have entertained a death-wish," I confessed to them in shamefaced honesty.

Then, joyfully, I related how the prayers of Christians, and the revelation given to Dr. Jarman about the book, had availed to bring about a transformation in my life during the past week. I told them the Holy Spirit and I were writing a book together, and that it was about suffering. Its title was, *What About Us Who Are Not Healed?*

I cited the example of our assistant pastor, a man of God if ever there was one, who was even now absent because of sickness. Ironically, he had just completed a series of Sunday school lessons on divine healing! I named several devout women in the church who time after time have come to the altar, been anointed with oil in the name of the Lord, elders' hands have been laid on them, and the prayer of faith given—and yet those women have gone home as sick in body as when they came. I mentioned my own afflictions.

"Why is this?" I asked. "What about us who are not healed?"

"Lord, You remember what followed. You took over the service, and testimony after testimony came forth." to my astonishment, one after another confessed to harboring, or having harbored in the past, the same wish to die. The longing to be free from the toil and the troubles, the pain and the sorrows of this life, had motivated many another death-wish besides mine.

Some said they had prayed that the Lord would take them home, for they felt they were of no use to themselves or anyone else. Sunday school teachers, pillars in the church, said this.

Various other spiritual matters came out in the testimonies too, of course. Finally one woman got up and said, "It seems that Satan has been spreading around the same lies to a lot of us, and we have fallen victim to them. Now that those lies have been exposed for what they are—the deception of the enemy—we can much easier stand against his wiles and overcome him."

A passing reference to my ulcer was responsible for one man's speaking up for the first time in all the years he has been attending the church. Never had he opened his mouth in testimony before, but last night he said:

"I had ulcers once. The Lord healed them when I was converted. At the same time, He delivered me from cigarettes. I have thanked Him and praised Him ever since."

"Remember," said the Holy Spirit, "I told you that many would identify with you, one way or another. This is part of the plan and purpose of our endeavor."

Then I recalled the closing words of the youngest person who spoke, a boy about sixteen. He said he had been listening to all the talk on the part of those older than he about not wanting to live. "Death is in God's hands," he declared. "Don't pray to die." He paused a moment. "You'll get your chance."

The entire congregation burst into laughter.

Toward the end of the long evening, a dear older lady stood up and said, "This has been the best sermon we've heard in the church for a long time!" The pastor, who had not preached a word, joined the rest of us in laughing heartily.

"Well, Lord, the Memorial Day holiday is drawing to a close, and I have to go to work at the store—where my husband has been all day. It is no holiday for us. Even death takes a holiday, they say. But we can't. Would You speak a final word to all of this?"

He responded with a Scripture:

"A word fitly spoken is like apples of gold in pictures of silver" (Prov. 25:11). Then He said, "In keeping with that, I will sum up your discourse with another proverb: 'A merry heart doeth good like a medicine' " (Prov. 17:22).

Impulsively, I blurted out the rest of the verse: "But a broken spirit drieth the bones." Then I added, "Lord, You have mended my spirit. Now how about breathing on my aching dry bones?"

VI

"As Christ Hath Suffered for Us in the Flesh"

(I Pet. 4:1)

God, speaking to Moses and Aaron, said, "All the congregation of Israel . . . shall take to them every man a lamb, according to the house of their fathers, a lamb for an house" (Exod. 12:3).

John the Baptist, seeing Jesus, said, "Behold the Lamb of God, which taketh away the sin of the world" (John 1:29).

I, seeing my little granddaughter, said, "No! Not my little lamb. . . !"

One morning there transpired a conversation between the Holy Spirit and myself which troubled me greatly. So much so that when it was over, I protested, "Lord, I am not going to write this down. It is too personal; it is too disturbing. Besides that, I don't understand the meaning of it. Especially its implication. That part I don't even want to understand. I can't bear to think about it. I want to forget it."

"Some things you do not understand now," said the Spirit.

37

"But I have said them to you so that when the time comes, you may remember that I told you of them."

"Lord, I have enough trouble just going about my business, living my life one day at a time," I argued. "Sufficient unto the day is the evil thereof."

"Sufficient also is My grace," said the Spirit.

Seven days later, He instructed me to write down what we had talked about. Here is my remembrance of that disquieting conversation:

It was very early in the morning, about five o'clock, when the Spirit awakened me and began in His usual way to impress upon my mind what He wanted me to write that day.

"Carmen," He said, "there is an aspect of suffering we have not yet touched upon."

"What is that, Lord?"

His hesitation caused me to sense that there was to be something different about this conversation. Then He asked, "What is your understanding of suffering that is called 'vicarious suffering'?"

"Well," I began, "vicarious suffering means that one person suffers in place of someone else, as a substitute, you might say. Jesus suffered in our stead, in order to bring beneficial results to us. We speak of it as the 'vicarious atonement.' "

"There is a Scripture," the Holy Spirit went on to say, "which reads, 'For unto you it is given in the behalf of Christ, not only to believe on him, but also to suffer for his sake."

Vaguely, I recalled that this was in Philippians somewhere near the end of the first chapter (29th verse).

"I thought You were going to bring up the Scripture in the first chapter of Colossians," I told my Teacher. "The one where Paul says he rejoices in his sufferings for other Christians. He calls it, 'filling up that which is lacking of the afflictions of Christ, suffering in his flesh for the sake of the body of Christ, which is the church' " (Col. 1:24 AP).

Without commenting upon this passage, and seeming to go in another direction, the Spirit said, "There is a Scripture that was spoken to Moses. In it God said, 'Sanctify unto me all the first-born, whatsoever openeth the womb among the children of Israel, both of man and of beast: it is mine' " (Exod. 13:2).

"Yes, Lord," I replied. "I have thought about that many times, since I am my mother's firstborn. Doesn't it mean a setting apart of the firstborn for holy use?"

"Sometimes it means more than that. Carmen," He went on, "you have frequently said that you feel you belong to the tribe of Levi."

"I use the name symbolically," I interposed blithely. "Of course, I'm not Jewish. But I know that I belong with the people who serve God in a priestly capacity, ministering spiritually to others."

"You have also said," the Spirit continued, "that you would be willing to offer your suffering unto God in a sacrificial manner if He were to ask that of you."

"Yes, that is true, Lord." My blithe spirit began to falter. "I cannot comprehend how my bodily suffering could avail spiritually, but if I were convinced that was Your will for me, I would try to comply with it."

Again the Holy Spirit appeared to swerve in tactic. "Abraham had a firstborn," He said.

"You mean Ishmael?" I asked.

"No. I mean his true seed, the firstborn of his wife Sarah—'thy son, thine only son Isaac,' as God Himself called him."

For a moment I couldn't imagine where the Holy Spirit was leading. Then all at once I felt cold. I reached over to turn up the electric blanket, but this trembling did not seem to be on the out-side of me. It was on the inside.

"What do You mean, Lord?" I whispered, my mind and heart struggling to reject the picture of that ancient scene on Mount Moriah—Abraham placing the wood on the altar for a burnt offering, taking the fire and the knife in his hand, and then binding Isaac, the child of the promise, and laying him upon that altar. Abraham stretching forth his hand and taking the knife to slay his son . . .

The Holy Spirit's answer provided a welcome interruption to

this disturbing recollection. "Abraham's willingness to sacrifice his only son," He replied calmly, "was a type, a foreshadow, of the actual sacrifice of another Son."

I was glad for this alteration in focus. "Yes, I know. God's only begotten Son, Jesus."

Jesus, the Lamb of God . . .

I have always loved the expression, "the lamb of God." Among the many pet names I used to give my daughter, Bonnie, was the name "lamb." I called her "my little lamb." When she gave birth to her first child, Carrie, the same term of endearment just naturally fell from my lips. The moment I saw Carrie's face—so tiny, so perfectly formed, like an exquisite cameo—I breathed a prayer of gratitude. "Thank You, Lord, for that lovely little lamb."

Five years have come and gone since I first beheld my grand-daughter through the glass in the hospital nursery. Five years in which my heart has entwined itself inextricably around that little life . . .

Suddenly a maze of confused, fear-filled thoughts crowded into my mind. My heart began to pound. "Lord!" I cried out, "You aren't inferring that Carrie will have to suffer for her family—a lamb for that household! Illness has already cast a pall over her life, even to major surgery. She's so fragile, so sweet, so precious. No, no! Please tell me I have not understood You aright. Fear so easily intrudes into my consciousness. I can't bear to think . . . " My voice trailed off.

"You do not like to recall the sacrifice Abraham offered to God," responded my Teacher. "Nor do you like to contemplate the suffering of the Son of God upon a cross of shame. You shrink even from the thought of sacrificial suffering for your own flesh and blood. Is that not so?" He questioned gently.

I had to admit it was. "Lord, it's humanly impossible not to shrink from it! I might be willing to sacrifice myself to save the life of my child or grandchild, but to be willing to see a child of mine suffer—to say nothing of *dying*—for others is beyond my capability."

What inner anguish it must have cost Abraham to perform

that act of faith, obedience, and absolute surrender, I marveled to myself. Yet how much greater must have been the pain in the heart of God when He saw His beloved Son mocked, spat upon, slapped, scourged, becoming sin for the sake of sinful man, and then crucified by the very ones He came to save. Only Divine Love—merciful and boundless—could possibly be willing to provide such a sacrifice.

"And to be Himself the sacrifice," interjected the voice of the Spirit, reading my thoughts.

"Oh, my God," I whispered, "the price that was paid for our redemption! Yet we who are redeemed seek to avoid pain and sacrifice and suffering for ourselves, and for those we love. We fear it, resent it, fight against it, and pray to be delivered from it! We cringe to think that we might ever be called upon to suffer for the sake of Christ—or for the sake of His body, which is the Church."

"There are many kinds of suffering," commented my Teacher, "but suffering itself is inevitable. The union of man's soul with God is inescapably bound up with pain and suffering."

"Lord, to me suffering seems such a terrible waste!"

"It is not suffering that is a waste," replied the Spirit. "It is you who waste it in fear, self-pity, and resentment. Christ suffered for your justification. All suffering is costly. Do not waste what costs so much."

"I know that the kind of suffering Abraham underwent when he offered Isaac as a sacrifice to God far transcends my physical distress," I told Him half-apologetically. "But Abraham's suffering was turned to gain. Mine just turns out a total loss."

"Suffering and trials are means of grace which God uses to sanctify His people," answered the Spirit. "Paul suffered the loss of all things that he might gain Christ."

This caused me to fall silent for a time. After some moments of reflection, I remarked, "Not many of us Christians are like Paul, who rejoiced that he suffered, especially for the sake of others. We want to know Christ—oh yes!—but we don't want to know the 'fellowship of His sufferings' or to 'be made conformable unto His death.' "

41

"There have been, and are, those souls who have prayed for and experienced a following of Christ's sufferings and a conformity to His death," my Guide informed me. "Remember this: suffering—whether it be for your own spiritual good, or for that of another—will never go unrewarded."

"I don't doubt that, Lord. But how can my physical suffering be for anyone's spiritual good?"

"Carmen," He said somewhat sternly, "you would do well to meditate on the sufferings of Christ and the gain they have brought you—rather than to dwell on your own sufferings, and on imagined sufferings you fear may befall your granddaughter. Daily follow, step by step, the will of God for your life, and forget yourself in the process. Obey the motions of grace, be patient under trial, be not fearful or troubled. The time will come when all things that I have said to you will be made clear, and you will understand how they have worked together for good."

"Lord, why can't that time be now?" I wanted to know. "You brought up the subject of vicarious suffering, sacrificial offering, consecration of the firstborn, substitution. But You haven't put the pieces together. Is this all You're going to say? Am I to be left to wonder and worry over what it implies?"

"To every thing there is a season," said the Spirit, "and a time to every purpose under the heaven. God does not tell everything to His children. He has some secrets that He keeps. Be thankful that He does. You would not want to know everything that awaits you in the future."

"No," I agreed, "not everything. Just the good things."

"In an earlier talk, you asked me why God did not tell Job that Satan was behind all of his troubles. I did not answer that question. Much takes place behind the scenes in the lives of many a soul that is not made known here. I have revealed enough to you for now."

As I pondered what the Holy Spirit had said, some other words echoed in the background of my mind. Moses had spoken them to God's people on the day that he was to die:

"The secret things belong unto the LORD our God. But those things which are revealed belong unto us, and to our children

42

forever, that we may do all the words of this law" (Deut. 29:29).

And then it seemed that the strains of an old hymn came to the foreground of my awareness: "Be not dismayed whate'er betide, God will take care of you. Beneath His wings of love abide. God will take care of you..."

So ended the conversation of the morning.

I do not pretend to understand it, nor have I pursued any further its application. That may be one of the secret things that belong to God. Someday He will make it plain to me. Until then, I leave the entire matter in His hands, trusting Him to make a fuller revelation when the time comes.

VII

"In Vain Shalt Thou Use Many Medicines"

(Jer. 46:11)

The lucky customer said, "We won a prize—a prize we don't need, a prize I don't want."

The unlucky Carmen said, "Oh that I might win the prize of health!"

The apostle Paul said, "That I might win Christ . . . the prize of the high calling of God" (Phil. 3:8 AP, 14).

For the last few days, I have been typing and editing what has been written so far. "I really like the work, Lord," I told Him, "but I certainly could do a better job without these all-day headaches that plague me so often. Like the one I had yesterday. I could hardly see. My face was puffy around the eyes. I looked awful. Felt worse. Sinus headache in the front, migraine on the side and in the back."

"Do you have the headache today?" He inquired.

"No."

"How is your leg?"

"Much better," I replied. "I can walk in a normal manner now."

"Some suffering does pass then, does it not?"

"True," I conceded grudgingly. "But these headaches will be back! And as for my leg—when pain lets up in one part of my body, I start hurting somewhere else."

"Perhaps we should change the title of this book to *The Power of Negative Thinking*," commented the Spirit.

I smiled. "I guess I have gotten into the habit of expecting the worst. That is some more of my dross that needs to go. Instead of dwelling on yesterday's headache, and dreading the possibility of another one tomorrow, I should be rejoicing that I don't have one today."

"What do you do about these headaches?" the Spirit asked.

"Lord, what can I do about them? You know my system will not tolerate strong drugs. I'm even allergic to aspirin. I take a mild tablet that is supposed to relieve sinus congestion and headache."

"Does it take away the pain?"

"No, it doesn't. The caffeine in it accelerates my pulse, over-stimulates me, leaving me exhausted the next day; and the antihistamine upsets my stomach."

"Then why take it?"

"Lord, I am the one that is always asking 'why?' " I pointed out. "Why must I have all these headaches? They're just too much."

"It is possible," acknowledged the Spirit, "to have too much of anything."

"You can't have too much of a good thing," I countered.

"Can't you?" He challenged. Then He reminded me of a conversation I had with one of our customers the previous day. She and her husband had attended a fund-raising dinner, and had won the grand door prize of the evening—a brand-new Lincoln Continental automobile!

When I congratulated her on this good fortune, she scoffed indifferently, with a tinge of boredom, "Congratulations? What for? We needed another car like we need a hole in the head."

To myself I agreed—for they already owned two new Cadillacs. "But aren't you thrilled over winning?" I questioned in

45

amazement. "Aren't you excited at all?"

"No," she answered with disarming frankness. Then her voice took on a note of animation. "Now if the prize had been something else, like a diamond necklace, for instance, I might have gotten excited about that!"

"Why don't you sell the Continental," I suggested, "and buy what you want?"

"Because all I really want is a diamond necklace," she replied, "and my husband won't let me buy that." Then, with a shrug of her shoulders, the unenthusiastic "lucky winner" left the store, got into her Cadillac Eldorado and drove away.

"A diamond necklace!" I repeated to myself, shaking my head in disbelief. I would have been overjoyed to have won a new automobile of whatever kind, but as for wanting a diamond necklace, I couldn't care less.

"Oh well, everything is relative," I murmured philosophically. "Those that have, get. And what they get, sometimes they don't even want." In retrospect I saw that the Holy Spirit was right, as always. One can have too much, even of a good thing.

"Except when it comes to health," I stated, resuming my conversation with the Lord.

"What did the apostle John say about health?" asked the Spirit.

My memory of the verse to which He referred was a little hazy, so I turned to my Bible and read it aloud: "Beloved, I wish above all things that thou mayest prosper and be in health, even as thy soul prospereth" (III John 2).

There was silence for a few minutes while I meditated upon the words of this Scripture. If the blessing of material prosperity and bodily health was the foremost wish of the apostle John for the particular saint to whom this letter was addressed, then that person probably was in need of both. Just as I was. Yet my soul was indeed prospered. That fact could not be overlooked either.

Suddenly I realized that perhaps I was guilty of more than the negative outlook for which the Spirit had admonished me. Perhaps I was as lacking in enthusiasm and thankfulness for my soul's prosperity and health, as was the customer of the material blessings she possessed. It was not a comfortable thought.

"Lord," I said, "You have been very good to me in many ways; and I have fallen far short of the standard of 'rejoicing evermore,' and 'in everything giving thanks.' I am terribly ashamed. I must again ask Your forgiveness."

My voice dropped to a fervent whisper. "Thank You, Lord, for the material prosperity that I possess, for the health of body and mind that I do have, and for the rich spiritual bounty that You have bestowed upon me. The latter alone so greatly exceeds any Lincoln Continental, Cadillac Eldorado, or diamond necklace that there isn't the slightest comparison— And one more thing, Lord," I said.

"What is that?" He asked.

"Lord, I love You," I told Him simply, with all the earnestness in my being.

"Would you love Me more if I healed you—healed you of everything?"

This startled me, causing me to stop abruptly and reflect upon His question. What was my honest answer to that? I was sure that the Lord, who discerns the thoughts and intents of the heart, already knew the answer—no doubt better than I did. But He wanted me to see it for myself. The only truthful response I could give Him was, "I don't know, Lord."

"If you were to be instantly and completely healed," He continued, "is it possible that you would be so busy rushing around, doing all the things that you like to do, that there would be little reason to turn to Me, and little time to spend with Me?"

"Oh Lord, I wouldn't do that!" I avowed. "I would rather have You than all this world has to offer. I love this closeness with You more than anything."

"More than healing?"

We were back again where we started. Did I love the gifts more than the Giver?

"Are You asking me to give up my hope of being healed?" I inquired. "That was the state I was in at the beginning of the book when I was wallowing in my death-wish. Or are You testing me to see if I would voluntarily relinquish that hope in preference to fellowship with You? Couldn't I have both?"

Instead of giving me a direct answer, the Holy Spirit replied, "You say that you love the fellowship of this teaching-writing relationship more than anything. How much do you love Christ in the fellowship of His sufferings?"

"Lord, You know that I love Jesus," I quickly asserted in self-justification. "But when You ask how much I love the fellowship of His sufferings—that is a hard question. I am willing to bear some suffering, but couldn't I have just a little healing? Just a little more strength? Surely that would not be asking too much. My body is weak; and for all the work I am called upon to do, I need the strength of a horse."

"Would you like to look like a horse, have the mentality of a horse, the spiritual development of a horse, in order to have the horse's strength?"

I snickered—whinnied, you might say. "No, I wouldn't."

"The Scripture says that God delights not in the strength of the horse," remarked the Spirit (Ps. 147:10).

"It also says that 'wisdom is better than strength' " (Eccles. 9:16), I said, "and that 'the LORD is the strength of my life' " (Ps. 27:1).

"Is He?" the Spirit asked. "Is He the strength of your life?"

"Lord, if we couldn't ask each other questions, what would we do?" Then I told Him imploringly, "Lord, please don't ever leave me. Order my life as You deem best. Healed or not healed, I love You."

He answered, "I will never leave you, or forsake you. I am with you always. The steps of a good man—or woman—are ordered by the Lord; and he delighteth in his way."

The next time we talked, I again brought up my request for "just a little healing." I gave as my reason that a person who is sick much of the time is not a very attractive witness to the unsaved.

"What Scripture says that you must be in good health to be a witness to the unsaved?" asked the Spirit.

I couldn't think of a single Scripture. I knew that the most

48

eminent of all witnesses—the apostle Paul—was not in perfect health. He suffered many things in his body and in his life. Yet he wrote to the church at Rome, "I consider that the sufferings of this present time are not worth comparing with the glory that is to be revealed to us" (Rom. 8:18 RSV).

Paul testified to the saints at Philippi, "For the sake of Christ Jesus my Lord, I have suffered the loss of all things, and count them as refuse" (Phil. 3:8 AP & RSV).

He told the Corinthians that he had been scourged five times, stoned once until he was dragged out of the city as dead, beaten with rods three times, endangered many times by perils of all kinds on land and sea. He said he had lived with weariness and pain and sleepless nights. Frequently he was hungry and thirsty and without food. Often he shivered with the cold, not having enough clothing to keep warm (II Cor. 11:24-27).

In circumstances like these, his health could not possibly have been good. Yet he proclaimed triumphantly that he took pleasure in infirmities for Christ's sake, even glorying in them!

There came to my mind the words of another distinguished witness—Peter, the apostle—who also must have suffered much in this life. He exhorted believers to stand true in all kinds of suffering:

"Beloved, do not be surprised at the fiery ordeal which comes upon you to prove you, as though something strange were happening to you. But rejoice in so far as you share Christ's sufferings, that you may also rejoice and be glad when his glory is revealed" (I Pet. 4:12, 13 RSV).

Peter concluded his testimony with this promise:

"And after you have suffered a little while, the God of all grace, who has called you to his eternal glory in Christ, will himself restore, establish, and strengthen you" (I Pet. 5:10).

I thought of those who "were tortured, cruelly mocked and scourged, chained and imprisoned, stoned, sawn asunder, tempted, slain with the sword . . . being destitute, afflicted, tormented, of whom the world was not worthy . . . " (Heb. 11:35-38 AP & KJV). They suffered unspeakably, and were not healed or delivered. If they had waited until they were in good health to witness to the unsaved, they would have done very little witnessing. Did they lack faith for healing or deliverance? No. The Bible plainly states:

"All these, though well attested by their faith, did not receive what was promised, since God had foreseen something better for us, that apart from us they should not be made perfect" (Heb. 11:39 RSV).

When I recalled all of this, I said—very sheepishly—to the Holy Spirit, "I retract my request for healing, and my reason that a sick person cannot be a good witness."

"You are not wrong in asking or hoping for healing," replied my Teacher. You are even scriptural in 'being always ready to give an answer and a reason for the hope that is in you.' "

The Spirit continued to speak. "I want to bring to your remembrance an incident that took place in the early days of our communion together. Your love for the Word then was so great that you read it standing up at your kitchen sink."

"I had to read standing up," I reminded Him. "My sciatica was so bad I couldn't sit down! Yet I couldn't keep away from the study of Your Word."

"Do you recall the particular passage I quickened to you one day when your Bible lay on the drainboard, open to the fifth chapter of Romans?"

"I'll never forget it, Lord," I responded appreciatively. "That was when the only Bible I had was the Revised Standard. But I am so glad I had that version, for in my opinion it translates that passage much better than the King James does:

" 'Therefore, since we are justified by faith, we have peace with God through our Lord Jesus Christ. Through him we have obtained access to this grace in which we stand, and we rejoice in our hope of sharing the glory of God.

" 'More than that, we rejoice in our sufferings, knowing that suffering produces endurance, and endurance produces character, and character produces hope.

" 'And hope does not disappoint us, because God's love has been poured into our hearts through the Holy Spirit which has been given to us' " (Rom. 5:1-5 RSV).

That same Holy Spirit now said to me, "Carmen, engrave the truth of those words in your heart, as well as in your mind. You rejoice in your hope of sharing the glory of God. Learn to rejoice also in your suffering, for it can indeed produce character. And character, as you yourself have often said, is of more value than healing."

"Yes, Lord; I firmly believe that. But isn't there another way, an easier way to produce it?"

"Are we going back to our many questions?" He asked.

"Well, Lord, there are a lot of questions in the Bible," I said defensively. "In one of my study Bibles, it says there are 3294 of them! And by far the most questions in any book are in the book of Job—329. With all his suffering, I certainly can see the reason for his asking so many questions."

"The Lord asked quite a few of Job," commented the Spirit.

"Yes, I know," I replied. "He asked 84 of them, to be exact. I did that bit of research myself—had to use my adding machine to do it. Since we have been writing this book, You must have asked me as many questions as You did Job!"

"I try to be consistent," said the Holy Spirit.

Laughing out loud, I exclaimed: "Lord, I love Your sense of humor!" Then, in a more serious vein, I added, "Lord, I love You."

VIII

"We Have Been in Pain"

(Isa. 26:18)

The Spirit asked, "What is the final answer to the
   problem of suffering?"
I said, "Lord, You've got me!"
The Lord said, "I will keep you." That was His final
   answer to the problem of suffering.

It was over, I thought.

Abruptly—without any notice—the warm, intimate, daily
companionship I had enjoyed with the Holy Spirit had come to
an end. One morning I awakened and realized He was not there.
At least not in the teaching-writing fellowship so treasured by
His pupil.

The heavenly Presence—which during the past weeks had
been lavishly bestowed upon me purely as a gift, without any
seeking or effort on my part—was now withdrawn, moved
back. Oh, I knew that He would still be with me, even in me, but
not in the same way. Not with the same degree of intensity or
constancy. Henceforth, I would have to seek Him out, call upon

Him, wait upon the Lord—the way things were before the book was started.

As He had come, so had He gone. I had not bidden Him enter my life in the manner that He had, nor could I have stayed His leave.

I thought back to our last conversation, not knowing at the time that it was the last. My closing words, I recalled, had been: "I love You." If it had to end—and of course it did—I was glad it had ended that way.

Then it struck me—

Never once had He said those words to me! Not once had He said, "I love you." Yet I had to acknowledge the fact that He had wrapped me in Divine Love all the while. He had enfolded me in a kind of spiritual cocoon. Now, inevitably, my soft warm cocoon was dissolved, and I was left to go about the daily routine on my own.

I felt sad and lonely. Tears welled up in my eyes, but resolutely I brushed them aside. There was a task to be done. "His part of our work on the book is completed," I said to myself. "But there remains for me the assignment of putting it into editorial form."

Though our discourse had been mostly conversation, nevertheless, underneath that simple dialogue lay deep truths which my mind and spirit had sensed without fully grasping. Now I knew that God expected me to digest them, meditate upon them, and pass them on to others, incorporating them into my life as I did so.

Strange, that He had not "lectured or sermonized," as man might have done. We had just talked together. Even so, being visited by the Lord in such a marvelous way had changed me. I was not the same person who had begun the book. Then I was at my lowest point, physically, mentally, and spiritually. Now I was stronger in all ways.

As many of the things that had been said kept coming back, I recognized the method that the heavenly Teacher had used. It was the very method I employ with my little five-year-old granddaughter, having found it to be the most efficacious way of teaching.

We just talk, and I ask her questions. She often gives me excuses, evasions, and complaints against her little brother. But after her self-defenses come down, she sees for herself where the real trouble lies. She puts her own finger on the sore spot, and in her sweet childish way admits the truth, even though it does not put her in the most favorable light.

Then I give her love, and we go on our way.

Yes, the Lord knew what He was doing all the time. To the smallest detail . . .

How appropriate that the Christians who prayed for me were in Arlington, Virginia—the place of our national cemetery! With my death-wish, I was doing all I could to cooperate with the devil to put me in the cemetery, too. Job spoke about "worms destroying his body." I couldn't wait for the worms—I was doing their work ahead of time, destroying my own body. How foolish!

My morbid thoughts had invited that dream about my mother, which was clearly a Satanic impersonation of her and the conditions surrounding her. Some of the devil's wiles are such poor counterfeits, they are just too obvious.

But God, ignoring all this, went right ahead with His plan and purpose. He gave the revelation about the book and confirmed it to me—after my willingness to obey Him was forthcoming. He always respects our freedom of choice, our right to say yes or no, even to Him. He equipped me with the Holy Spirit as Teacher and Helper, and poured out living water through me.

To my complaint about increased physical pain, the Spirit used the Scripture about death's sting and the grave's victory. At the time, it had seemed totally irrelevant, but it proved to be the most fitting place to begin.

How it had opened up other Scriptures! And then to discover that all of them concealed as well as revealed the Lord Jesus Christ, the greatest Promise ever made, the most all-inclusive Gift ever given!

Looking back, I saw how the Holy Spirit had drawn out of

me—and heaven knows, it wasn't difficult—my negativity, my fears, my putting the blame on others, my resentment of my lot in life, my exaggeration of its toil and drudgery, my envying those women who have things much easier—or so I imagine.

And oh, the excuses!

Convincing myself that I could not be a good witness for Him because of my many ailments—though I was an ever-ready witness to all those ailments.

The complaints . . . the evasions . . . the self-centeredness . . .

Being disappointed in the Lord for not healing me, unmindful of all the saints who have walked before me suffering a hundredfold more than I. Forgetting the supreme sufferer of all, my blessed Redeemer, Jesus—who made Himself a sacrificial offering for my sins, my sicknesses, and my sanctification.

I saw how adroitly the Spirit had given me the opportunity of making a sacrifice in my own life by relinquishing that most cherished possession—self-gratification. All too apparent was my willingness to accept the sacrifice of the Lamb of God, but my unwillingness to even think of any kind of sacrifice for "my little lamb."

Other traits had revealed themselves . . .

My wavering over whether I desired healing more than the Healer, the gifts more than the Giver; hoping to share His glory, but wanting to escape any share in His sufferings.

Oh, in retrospect, it was all there! My shortcomings were unveiled in all their stark ugliness.

Yet His goodness was there, too. The gentleness of His correction; even His rebuke had tenderness in it. There was protection and transformation in the soft cocoon that He had spun around me to insulate me from the world.

I recalled how I would turn on the news, but soon would turn it off in disinterest. Why should I listen to things of the world, when I could be holding conversation with the Lord? Because of His mercy, I was moved with compassion as I viewed others, instead of being critical of them. Business worries no longer bothered me, the same ones that had previously sent me into a panic. My own pain receded in importance. His loving-kindness had culminated in the promise of a victorious outcome. He had confirmed that promise in the written Word of God.

He had done all these things, but He had not healed me.

Not physically, that is. Spiritually, He had more than made me whole. He had cured my unhealthy mental state, remedied my emotional wounds, and restored to me the joy of my salvation. "Made whole . . . cured . . . remedied . . . restored . . . " Is that not healing?

What is bodily healing compared to that? When two-thirds of me—my soul and spirit, the real me, the only part I will be taking with me—is healed, should I complain because bodily health was left out? Perhaps we greatly overrate healing. Physical healing, like physical life, comes to an end. But that which has been wrought in the soul and spirit never ends. It belongs to eternity.

To me it is significant that the Holy Spirit had not given pat answers to anything.

Some teachers convey the impression that if you are born-again, baptized in the Holy Ghost, walking in the Spirit, reading the Bible, praying, and having faith—all will be well. You will be healed and prospered, and live happily ever after.

There are other Christians who consider that sickness, pain, suffering, financial loss, unanswered prayer are so negative they do not want even to recognize their existence. They feel that somehow these things refute everything for which they stand. They love to talk and hear about miracles of healing, but to those who are not healed, they have little to say. That subject they prefer to sweep under the rug. If confronted with the issue, they usually dismiss the Christian sufferer as one lacking in faith, living in sin, or bound by the devil. To put all the blame on others, even on Satan, is equally wrong.

The simple truth is that there are no pat answers to suffering and healing, and the why and the wherefore of it. Each case is as unique as the person, and there are many factors that have a part in each life.

No one has everything. Those who seem to have are often unsatisfied, ungrateful, and unhappy. The acquisition of things that make life better, even the gaining of perfect health, is not the goal and purpose of living.

Physical healing is not the ultimate gift of the Holy Spirit. Healing does not merit preeminence in spiritual value. The Lord showed me that I myself place other things far above it. I do seek it, earnestly pray for it, and greatly appreciate it—but it does not have the number-one position on my prayer list.

Just the other day—this was some time after my heavenly Teacher had made His unexpected departure—the Holy Spirit proved this to me.

I was sitting under the dryer in the beauty parlor reading, when suddenly He spoke again. "Carmen," He said, "is there something I could give you that is more important to you than healing?"

Immediately, emphatically, unequivocally I replied, "Oh yes, Lord, there is!"

That was sufficient and positive proof to me that healing does not occupy the top place when it comes to my priorities, or what I really want.

This is not to minimize pain and affliction. I know only too well that suffering—in whatever degree—is not a pleasant experience. It can blacken the horizon and choke off happiness. Truly, it is "a lonely business," as one of the recent saints among us said. I would not choose it for my path of life. In and of itself, it is anything but elevating. It may refine, but its refining is through the fire.

Someone has said, "Faith can stagger on the mystery of pain." I know from bitter experience that faith can not only stagger in the face of intense and prolonged pain and suffering, but it can fall, and even grovel in the dust of despair and defeat.

Yet I also know from experience, and from the inspiring example of those with whom I am personally acquainted—as well as those of whom I have read or heard—that faith can rise triumphantly and victoriously in the very midst of pain. With God's help, we can live with it, if necessary—and better than that, we can live above it, if we have the character and the spiritual maturity to do it.

Suffering can be transcended. It is not easy to transcend it. For people like me, it is downright impossible without the help of the Lord. But, with Him, it can be done. I haven't reached the place where I can rejoice in my sufferings, or glory in my infirmities, but I have come to the place—thank God!—where they no longer have dominion over me.

Aside from the causes of suffering—sin, Satan, self, heredity, environment, circumstance, old age; aside from the sources of healing—supernatural, natural, or remedial; aside from whether or not any of the suffering is sacrificial or substitutionary—some other truths remain indelibly inscribed in my consciousness. Here is my attempt to summarize them:

Regardless of the cause, regardless of the cure, God is Lord over all causes and all cures. He is sovereign. He runs the universe His way and according to His timing. He has his reasons for intervening in the lives of those who receive miracles of healing; He has His reasons for withholding healing intervention in the lives of those whom He does not heal.

God did not give His reasons to Job as he sat among the ashes of a rubbish pile, scraping his boils with a piece of broken pottery. God did not answer Jesus as He hung on the cross and cried out, "Why?" If He did not give His reasons to a man "blameless and upright, one who feared the Lord and turned away from evil"; if He did not answer His only begotten Son—then God is not going to make a full disclosure now of the problem of suffering to you or to me, or to anyone else.

Better, however, than giving a reason is what God did.

To Job, He revealed Himself so clearly that the sufferer could say at the end of his trial, "I have heard of thee by the hearing of the ear; but now mine eye seeth thee" (Job 42:5). God not only gave Job a revelation of His presence and His grandeur, but He gave him twice as much materially as he had before. He blessed the end of his life more than it was blessed at the beginning, when he seemed to have everything.

God answered Jesus by raising Him from the dead, highly

exalting Him, seating Him at the right hand of the throne of the Majesty in heaven. Not only did He glorify Him with the glory He had before the world was, but God gave Jesus a name that is above every name. And He is going to give Him a kingdom over which to reign, a kingdom that shall have no end.

Dear fellow-sufferer, when you attend a meeting in which many are miraculously healed, never forget that the larger number do not receive healing. We who are not healed are not the minority anywhere. We are the majority. But we are in good company. Even illustrious company, as may be seen by glancing over the lives of saints of the past.

Did you ever stop to realize that if Job had not suffered, he wouldn't be in the Bible? He would have lived and died, and we would never have known anything about him. But because of his suffering, he is immortalized forever in human history, secular as well as sacred.

Suffering is not irreconcilable with a loving Father, a holy God. Affliction is permitted in order to purify us, so that we might see God in all His splendor, and ourselves as we really are. When this happens, we will repent of our pride and self-centeredness, as did Job in dust and ashes.

God has not abandoned us. His purpose in allowing suffering is not to get us down. *His purpose is to build us up. He has something better for us.* If healing was for our greatest good, the Lord would heal us. He is molding us, reshaping us, to conform us to the likeness of Christ, and that often entails suffering.

God wills that each of us be made whole. But remember— spiritual wholeness is the greatest blessing, the greatest healing of all. If we set the Lord always before us, permitting nothing to move us; if we seek to know Him more fully, instead of seeking personal benefits—His will shall be done in us. Let us resign ourselves—deliberately relinquishing our desires and our will—to Him.

If we do, we can rest assured that He will heal us in His own perfect way, in His own perfect timing. Should He, in divine wisdom and sovereignty, withhold bodily healing in this life, we can still enjoy a better healing now and in the life to come. An eternal healing.

In the meanwhile, let us learn all we can from our suffering—obedience, patience, compassion, endurance, humility, and above all else, trust. Some of us may not be able to say, "Though he slay me, yet will I trust in him" (Job 13:15). But all of us can learn to know the Lord better by trusting Him today, and tomorrow, and the day after.

We can change our perspective regarding suffering. Instead of seeing it as an adversity of limitation, misery, and defeat, we can view it as an opportunity for growth, joy, and triumph. Believe it or not, potentially it is all that—and more.

If we are to gain the victory, the Lord must become more important to us than ourselves, our comfort, our temporal earthly life. We have to look beyond ourselves, and keep our eyes fixed upon God.

High-sounding platitudes about suffering from those who have never been there, wear thin in a hurry. But oh, there is solid strength in yielding our will, our affections, our mind, and our spirit to the Lord! There is peace in the knowledge that if He allows the body to suffer, it is for the purpose of working out something that is of far more consequence and lasting value than physical health.

Someday we will be glad for the path we had to walk. Even now, we who are not healed, or are only partially healed, can say with Job, "He knows the way that I take; when he has tried me, I shall come forth as gold" (Job 23:10RSV).

Character that is spun out of suffering can become silk, pure and golden. And what had been a wormlike creature within can emerge with shining wings to soar above all that is of the earth. No matter what happens to the body—by the grace of God, the soul can wing its flight upward into the light of heaven.

He designed it that way.

One morning when my typing and editing of the book was almost finished, I lay in bed reflecting on former conversations with the Holy Spirit. I had not yet fully recovered from my sense of loss, so sweet, so sheltered, so constant had been my fellowship with Him. Tears of sadness began to seep from my eyes.

In the stillness of the morning, and not at all certain that He was listening—or even there—I whispered, "Lord, could I ask You just one last question?"

There was silence for a moment. Then once more I heard His gentle voice.

"What is it?" He inquired.

"Why didn't You ever say to me, 'I love you'?"

Again there was a pause before He answered.

"I did say it," He replied. "I said it on Calvary. I repeated it many times as you sought Me in the Word and in prayer. I encompassed you with love as we wrote the book. But now I will say it plainly—'Carmen, I love you.' "

My tears really did begin to flow then! But these were happy tears.

And I knew why Jesus called Him the Comforter.

Part Two — The Cure

Webster defines cure:
"Spiritual charge; care of souls. A method of medical treatment. An act of healing. Means of removal of disease or evil. A remedy. A process."

The physician observes:
"Jesus cured many of diseases and plagues and evil spirits; and on many that were blind he bestowed sight" (Luke 7:21 AP & RSV).

The apostle advises:
"Let those who suffer according to God's will do right, and entrust their souls to a faithful Creator" (I Pet. 4:19 RSV).

IX
"I Will Take Sickness Away"

(Exod. 23:25)

I said, "It's ended. The book is finished. That's all there
   is."
My critics said, "It's incomplete. Resume your work."
The Lord said, "You have seen for yourself that I
   have talked with you. Continue in what you have
   learned and have firmly believed, knowing from
   whom you learned it" (Exod. 20:22 AP & RSV ; II Tim.
   3:14 RSV).

Several months passed after the first part of the book came to
a conclusion. The Lord taught me many things during that time,
in a different manner than He taught before. Some excellent
spiritual books enriched my understanding. Other people—
including my critics—also taught me. All of this was more of
God's way of doing things.

   The flow of life was a teacher, too . . .

   After the writing stopped, I enjoyed a brief period of freedom
from sickness and affliction. But very soon I was again brought

low—this time by a chest virus. Bordering on pneumonia, and racked with coughing spells night after night, allergic to any suppressant (even so small an amount as is contained in a cough drop), I was utterly miserable.

The diet required to deal with the virus (citrus juices in particular) caused my ulcer, the hiatal hernia, the colitis, cystitis, and arthritis—all five conditions—to flare up. On top of that, a constant toothache plagued me.

So, here I was, back in bed where the book started. The warm half-and-half at regular intervals, the heating pad, the pain, and the weakness made up the same old familiar pattern. And I knew full well from past experience that the milk diet would soon bring on a recurrence of sinusitis and its accompanying violent headaches.

"It's a vicious circle," I told the Lord.

But this time I did not give up and wish for death. I resisted the temptation to become negative. I continued to pray for healing, and many other Christians prayed with me. Through it all, I deliberately practiced praising the Lord. I did not praise Him for the virus—that would be attributing to God the work of the devil. But I thanked Him for His presence with me, His strength and His help. I loved Him, and trusted Him to do with me as He saw fit, according to His plan and purpose for my life.

Still I was not healed.

Yet, strangely enough, this time it didn't seem to matter. One day in the very midst of my physical misery, I realized I was happy. Happy inside, happy in my soul. How could such a thing be? I started singing gospel songs, one after another. In between, I was laughing. What an incongruous sight I must have been— sick as a dog, weak as a cat, propped up on pillows—singing and laughing!

"Why am I singing and laughing, Lord?" I asked Him. "I should be complaining and feeling sorry for myself. What's come over me?"

He answered in two words: "I have."

For a moment, I was stunned. My mind groped for the meaning of what He said. From somewhere in the background of my brain, the most peculiar words were sounding: "The Holy Ghost shall come upon thee, and the power of the Highest shall overshadow thee . . . " (Luke 1:35).

"Lord," I whispered, "You surely aren't implying that . . . anything holy . . . can be born in me, and come forth . . . " My voice trailed off.

"If it hasn't already been born in you," He replied, "we've both been wasting our time."

"Why didn't You come over me sooner, Lord?"

"I did," He said. "But you chose to let worry, fear, discouragement, and self-pity rule over you instead. You could have chosen wholly to trust in Me, if you had so willed."

"Did I really *choose* those negative forces? They just seemed a natural reaction, simply human nature."

"They are part of your human nature," He noted matter-of-factly, "and it is that nature with its instincts and disposition, its desire for self-gratification and earthly pursuits that must be put off."

"Where do I begin, Lord—this putting-off procedure?"

"Humility is a good place to begin, and a good place to remain. Be clothed with humility, for God resisteth the proud and giveth grace to the humble."

"What is humility?" I asked my Teacher. "Is it an external behavior?"

"Humility is not an outer attitude or act. It is an inner spirit of lowliness," replied the Spirit. " 'Blessed are the poor in spirit' is the first requisite Jesus named when He instructed His disciples regarding the qualities they must have to develop and perfect Christian character. Humility is the highest virtue, the root of every virtue, and man's first duty before God."

"No wonder then that the first of the seven deadly sins is pride," I remarked.

"Pride is fatal to spiritual progress," He answered.

Another question occurred to me. "Does one display the sin of pride when one is self-centered?" I asked.

"Both are egocentric," stated the Spirit. "The only difference is in degree."

I laughed. "I have a good illustration of this, Lord. One night I was sitting next to a Christian friend when she inquired about my book—how I was coming along with it. I began to tell her, no doubt with a shade of pride."

"To say nothing about a shade or two of self-centeredness," interposed the Spirit.

Reluctantly acquiescing, I went on with my story. "It took just about a minute to see that she was not very interested in me and my work, so I decided to see if what the Lord had to say would interest her. I started to tell her some of the marvelous truths that had been imparted to me as I wrote. But in less than a minute, I noticed her eyes were straying around the room, and I knew her attention was elsewhere. Abruptly I ceased talking about myself or the Lord's teaching. Instead, I said to her, 'You're in the book.' "

" 'What!' she exclaimed with a slight shriek. 'I'm in the book!' Instantly I had her full attention. Her eyes were riveted on me now, and they sparkled with excitement. 'What do you mean? What did you write about me?' She was listening with both ears."

I finished my illustration by saying, "Lord, suppose there had been an instrument to register genuine interest. On a ten-point scale, her interest in me would register about two points. What You revealed to me would register about one point. But interest in the fact that she herself was in the book would hit the top! Ten points immediately."

The Spirit paused slightly before responding. "On that ten-point scale of genuine interest, My rating was not too high, was it?" He observed.

"Oh, she really loves You, Lord," I hastily affirmed. "It's just that she isn't particularly interested in what You say to *me*. If You said the same thing to her, she would be thrilled to death and would get up in church and give a wonderful testimony about it."

"What if we were to measure you, Carmen? In comparing your genuine interest in others with your interest in yourself, would there be any disproportion there?"

"Not that much of a one!" I declared vehemently.

"Again it's only a matter of degree," He said. "That's why the axe must be laid at the root of the tree—the tree of the self-nature, the 'flesh' as the Scriptures term it."

"But interest in one's self is an inescapable human condition, isn't it?" I asked defensively.

"It is an obsession," He stated flatly. "Self-esteem, pride, absorption in self, desire for self-exaltation—what does that remind you of?"

"Lucifer's downfall," was my prompt reply.

"Yes," He said. "Pride can degrade the highest angel into a devil, but humility can raise fallen man to the thrones of angels. So you see why Jesus taught His disciples to deny self and to be centered in Him. Humble yourself under the hand of God, and He will exalt you in due time."

"Self-centeredness is actually a sickness, isn't it, Lord?" I asked.

"A malignant one," He answered.

"Deliver me from that affliction then, Lord!" I cried out.

"My purpose is to deliver you from all evil," He said, "and to guide you into all truth. As you desire and yield to God's will, submitting yourself to the necessary discipline and training, that purpose will be accomplished."

"You take away all kinds of sickness, don't You, Lord?" I asked hopefully.

"The Scripture promised that to those who serve and obey God."

My next remark came several minutes later. "Suffering and trials humble us, I know." To which the Holy Spirit replied, "Affliction is calculated to produce humility of spirit, particularly if one is to receive the blessing of advancement. God never elevates a person to great dignity without first trying him, proving him—testing his dedication, his powers of endurance and self-control."

"A spiritual shakedown, you might call it," I suggested.

"Paul called it a thorn in the flesh," said the Spirit.

"I've had several of those thorns, Lord—for a long time. And they haven't been removed. I guess I must need humbling badly. Well, one thing is for sure—my critics humbled me. So much so I quit writing entirely and decided not even to finish the book."

"Critics can be of real help if you let them," said the Holy Spirit, altering somewhat the focus of our conversation. "Certainly not everything they say is in accord with divine wisdom. It is important to discern between man's judgment and the clear leading of the Lord. But it is well to give courteous heed and consideration to the views of those who do not see things as you do."

"But there is so much controversy among believers—even between sincere and devoted Christians," I protested.

"There needn't be," replied my heavenly Teacher. "If each is seeking the truth, not merely interested in defending his own opinion, controversy can be of profit. However, another 'if' is imperative. *If* personal ego is subdued, it may be found that both viewpoints are true—partially true, at least. No individual or group has all the truth. Usually a higher truth needs to be discovered that will amplify as well as reconcile the divergent views."

"It's that second 'if' that causes the trouble with most Christians I've encountered," I declared knowingly. "They don't want to get their ego out of the way, and that opens wide the door for Satan to get into the act."

"Is your ego always out of the way, Carmen?" He inquired blandly.

"I'm afraid not," I confessed rather sheepishly. "Lord, I don't want to entertain—much less project—an exaggerated estimate of my own worth. But am I—" I hesitated, then meekly finished the question. "Lord, am I important to You?"

"Not a sparrow falls to the ground without your Father's knowing it," answered the Holy Spirit. "God does not overlook a single one of them. The very hairs of your head are numbered. Rest assured, you are far more valuable to Him than a flock of sparrows. Remember, your soul is important enough that Jesus gave His life to save it, and important enough that I have been sent to guide you in spiritual living and to work within you to build your Christian character."

"Thank You, Lord," I said gratefully. "Thank You. That really humbles me!"

My thoughts reverted to the picture of the way I was when the book began. "The death-wish scene; the complaint reaction to bodily suffering," I called it now.

In retrospect, I could see how I had demonstrated everything Webster listed when he defined "complaint," especially "expression of grief, pain, or resentment." Even to the words, "a formal allegation against a party." How I had recited all the facts intended to prove my case! They may have been unsupportable and insufficient, but I defended them on the basis that I was in good company in so doing. For had not David and Job done the same thing? And one of them was "a man after God's own heart," and the other "an upright man who feared God and stayed away from evil."

Suddenly I stopped short. Here was that old self-nature rising up again—the flesh justifying itself because other "good people" had similar tendencies and failings. No wonder Webster said complaint was "an ailment, a sickness, a disease." It's contagious!

"You know, Lord," I said aloud, "I learn a lot from the Bible, but I also learn a lot from the dictionary."

With a smile, I returned to the review of past events. In contrasting the death-wish complaint with the more recent singing-laughing reaction to the virus attack, I was struck by a vivid realization.

"Some progress has actually taken place in me!" I exclaimed with a note of triumph. "And thank God it has!"

"Yes," said my Companion, "He is the one to thank—though it is a mutual endeavor, a joint effort, when a child of His grows in grace and achieves a necessary overcoming in personal character."

"I can see something else now, too, Lord," I remarked joyfully. "Your hand has been upon me all the time! And it wasn't for evil, it was for good! You were helping me to gain victory over myself—my lower self, my human nature."

A few moments later I said to Him, "It's a funny thing, Lord. Among my many sins, I never considered pride to be one of them. I felt I could have used a little more of it, since a lack of self-confidence has handicapped me all my life. Yet now I see that while the manifestation of the flesh may take different forms—or degrees, as You put it—in various people, it's still flesh. It's still the lower nature rearing its ugly head. 'They that are in the flesh,' I quoted, 'cannot please God' " (Rom. 8:8).

A number of other Scriptures immediately rushed to the foreground of my consciousness: "In my flesh dwelleth no good thing" (Rom. 7:18). "The flesh profiteth nothing" (John 6:63). "Put on the Lord Jesus Christ, and make no provision for the flesh, to fulfill the lusts thereof" (Rom. 13:14 AP).

"Walk by the Spirit, and do not gratify the desires of the flesh. For the desires of the flesh are against the Spirit, and the desires of the Spirit are against the flesh" (Gal. 5:16,17 RSV). "Those who belong to Christ Jesus have crucified the flesh with its passions and desires" (Gal. 5:24 RSV).

"Lord," I went on with the voicing of my reflections, "pride might not be my most besetting sin, but I have plenty of self—human nature, carnality, the flesh. I have that ailment all right. My reaction to physical suffering certainly proves it. How many of those tests I flunked! I'm beginning to suspect that my suffering is not so much the test; it's my reaction to it that is the test!"

" 'In that, saidst thou truly,' " quoted the Spirit. Then He added, "Reaction is more revealing than action."

"You can say that again, Lord. I've seen people—when things don't go to suit them, or they don't get their way, or someone else doesn't do exactly what they want them to do—it's then that their real self is revealed. They show what they really are by their reaction to a given situation."

"Certain situations have been given to you, Carmen," said my Teacher. "In looking back upon them, what would you say was the victory to be gained from them? For what profit did God allow them to come your way?"

I opened my mouth to respond, and a horrible thought came out:

"Don't tell me that illness, infirmity, and affliction have been Your means of helping me to develop maturity of Christian character—to go on toward perfection and the fulfillment of Your purpose for my life! Don't tell me that!"

He didn't. He made no answer at all.

X
"And Delivered Him out of All His Afflictions"

(Acts 7:10)

I said, "Bodily illness is enough. I don't need business dif-
ficulties and family worries at the same time to add to
my trial."
The Bible said, "The trial of your faith is more precious
than gold....Add to your faith" (I Pet. 1:7 AP ; II
Pet. 1:5).
The poet said, "To added affliction He addeth His mercy;
To multiplied trials, His multiplied peace."

Right in the middle of my virus attack, to the existing physical
vexation, two new forms of suffering were added. These were
primarily emotional in nature, though the first one included
financial distress as well. It had to do with our business . . .

Prices commenced to soar all over the nation, and that spelled
bad news for the small grocery store. Dozens of our regular
customers deserted us for the discount houses. Sales dropped
alarmingly.

On top of that, the only reliable employee we had—our son-

74

in-law—graduated from college and took a supervisory position with a large company. We didn't blame him for this; there was no future for him with us. But because he had been our mainstay and right hand for so many years, his going left a tremendous hole in the store. My husband began to work thirteen to fourteen hours a day, six days a week—sometimes seven.

Troubles compounded.

Refrigeration equipment broke down, necessitating enormous repair bills. The hiring and training and putting up with various high school and college boys was a constant exercise in frustration and incompetence. The meat man, who had leased from us for twelve years, retired. My husband was afraid a new owner would jeopardize our grocery business. So, without my knowing a thing about it, and without his knowing a thing about the meat business, he bought the meat department himself, paying far more than it was worth.

This, in itself, was sufficient to give me another ulcer. And trying to run the meat department after he bought it provided an ideal set-up for both of us to have a heart attack or a stroke.

We attempted to sell the store. No one would have it. People these days don't want to work as hard as we do for as long hours and as little money.

"Only a fool would buy it," I told a Christian friend.

"Then we'll just have to pray that God will raise up a fool," she answered confidently.

In my opinion, the world was already full of them, but none came our way—at least not in the role of potential buyer. Our lease still had five years to go. It hung over our heads like a gigantic monster ready to devour us, and like a prison sentence to be served without possibility of parole.

Shortages of considerable size began to appear in our cash registers. An employee was found drinking on the job. A truck crashed into our parking-lot sign and shattered it, marking the third truck and the third time we had to go to all the trouble of having that sign fixed. Bad checks, dead-beat accounts, and expenses piled up; and the bank balance went down—to rock bottom. More customers left us. I worried over what I would do if my husband's health gave way, or he had to have surgery again as he had the previous year. Without anyone to take his place, this entire mess would fall on my shoulders.

Oh, it all combined to make up a particular kind of suffering that can only be understood by experience. And what a wretched experience to have! In a small business like ours, you are never free from responsibility and serious problems. They hound you all day and haunt you half the night.

While the actual crisis connected with the store came during my virus siege, I was aware that the business had been making me sick for a long time. Many a morning and many an afternoon on my way to work, I would drive up the alley breathing a fervent prayer, "Oh Lord, please let there be several cars in front of the store!" Then when I caught sight of the empty parking lot, my heart would sink and my stomach tighten.

If there were one or two cars there, I would say, "Thank You, Lord for those one or two customers. Bless them, prosper them, bring them back, and multiply them."

Yet, in spite of outward discouraging evidence, I struggled to praise and trust the Lord. Upstairs in my little cubbyhole office, I wrote down a verse of Scripture and taped it on the wall above the telephone. It read: "Blessed is the man that trusteth in the Lord, and whose hope the Lord is" (Jer. 17:7).

One day a customer's teenage daughter came upstairs to cash a large check. Her father is a doctor, and her usual surroundings had not prepared her for my office.

"Is this where you work?" she asked incredulously, looking at the dilapidated furnishings and cramped quarters. "How do you stand it?"

In a well-worn, martyr-like voice I replied, "I'm used to it."

What I should have done was to show her my little sign and tell her that because of that Scripture, exterior things didn't really bother me. But you see, they did.

On another occasion, our pastor's wife commented in regard to the demands the store constantly made upon me, "I don't see how you stand it!" This added a little more fuel to the fire of resentment I had permitted to burn inside me for years. A feeling of bondage, and a lengthy list of grievances against my husband for forcing me into this situation, were of long standing.

I wondered why the Lord didn't help us. Other Christians were prospered in business. I convinced myself I could trust Him a lot more if He would send a little good fortune our way for a change. Once in a while He did, and then I would look at that sign and say, "Yes, blessed is the man that trusts in the Lord."

Other times, when things looked especially bleak, I would look at those words "whose hope the Lord is" and—I'm ashamed to confess it—I was tempted to rip that sign off the wall. Thank God, I never could bring myself to do it.

"The day of the small businessman has long since passed," I would repeat to my poor husband for the umpteenth time.

"I know it has," he would respond in a listless voice. "But what can I do about it?"

I thought about the man who ran the automatic laundry where I used to take my clothes. His wife helped him in the business, though she had six children at home to care for as well. In my mind's eye, I could still see her, a thin, frail woman, sitting at those long tables, folding endless piles of clothes that had been taken out of the constantly running machines. She always looked as pale and washed-out as if she herself had been run through the laundry by mistake. While she was doing all that work in the back of the store, her husband was up front smoking a big cigar, taking the customers' money, and laughing and talking with them.

One day I came in, and the wife was no longer there. The husband was filling and unloading the big machines. Three of the children were folding the clothes. They told me that their mother had suffered a stroke and was left paralyzed and unable to speak a word. I never saw her again.

Shortly after that, the laundryman's business began to dwindle. "I used to have two kinds of days," he told me a few months later, "good days and bad days." He paused, then said with a weak laugh, "I still have two kinds of days—now I have bad days and *really* bad days!"

That was the way our own business was headed, I feared. I remembered the people from whom we purchased the store. This same business had given the husband a heart attack; and the wife—who sat in the broken-down chair I sit in, but not for as long as I have occupied it—reaped stomach ulcers from it.

"No wonder," I mumbled to myself as I worked on the profit-and-loss statement. "This is no kind of life! We can't go anywhere; we can't even have friends over. And we're barely eking out an existence. Dear Lord, what about the promise in the Scripture to the righteous man that 'whatsoever he doeth shall prosper'?"

"What about it?" the Holy Spirit interrupted my mutterings.

"Why don't You honor it for us?" I wanted to know.

"I have not seen the righteous forsaken, nor his seed begging bread," He replied quietly.

"Well, I have seen Jack begging to buy bread from one of the bread men who won't bother delivering to our store because we're too small. He has to try to catch the bread man every morning in the parking lot of a supermarket to get any bread. What about that?"

"Man does not live by bread alone," was the Spirit's answer.

Against the backdrop of business misery and the physical affliction of a chest virus, something else happened. A third form of suffering made its debut . . .

It was Sunday evening, and I was propped up in bed wondering which was sicker—me or the business. By this time, the singing-laughing reaction had faded somewhat. My husband was still at the store cleaning the meat cases and making out the grocery order. The world, the flesh, and the devil had successfully prevented both of us from being in church morning or evening. Suddenly the phone rang.

Untangling the cord of the heating pad, and trying to stifle a coughing fit, I reached across the bed and picked up the receiver.

"Mother, I'm awfully sick, and I don't know what to do," the voice of our daughter sounded across the wire.

"Oh no, not more sickness!" I groaned to myself. "What seems to be the trouble?" I asked her, fear clutching at me.

"I've got a high fever and abdominal pains."

"Have you called a doctor?"

"We don't have any doctor except the children's pediatrician, and I can't get him. It's Sunday night, and all I get is the exchange."

"You had better go to a hospital then, dear," I advised her. Inwardly, I wondered if that was the best thing to do, or if such expense was necessary. "The emergency physician will be able to tell whether it's intestinal flu, or possibly your appendix, or something else," I reasoned.

All that night I worried and prayed and coughed, sleeping fitfully. Late the next morning, she telephoned frantically from the hospital.

"Mother, you've got to help me! This crazy doctor has given me all kinds of tests, a barium enema, and he still doesn't know what's wrong. Now some other doctor is getting ready to operate on me. Vince isn't here—he's with the children. My neighbor tells me this doctor is a butcher—has a terrible reputation. Get me out of here quick! Please!"

I was twenty-five miles away from where she was—and shaking with fright, nervousness, sickness, and weakness—but I told her I would try to call a reputable doctor in our area and ask him to examine her.

This proved to be no easy task. However, after innumerable phone calls, interspersed with desperate prayers, I succeeded in getting her out of that hospital and transported to another. Once she was in the competent hands of our own surgeon, I collapsed back in bed to await his verdict. My praying resumed, and I telephoned other Christians, asking them to pray with me.

The next development was not long in coming. Appendicitis was suspected, and emergency surgery scheduled. During the operation, it was discovered that the appendix had ruptured and peritonitis had set in.

"Your daughter would have been dead in less than ten hours," the doctor informed me after it was all over. "Because of the peritonitis, she will have to stay in the hospital several days longer than is normally required. For three of those days, there will be tubes down her nose and intravenous feeding; and she will be a very sick girl."

As things turned out, more trouble lay ahead . . .

Bonnie was home from the hospital less than a week when she was again stricken with sharp abdominal pains and vomiting. The doctor ordered her to return to the hospital. This time the diagnosis was an intestinal obstruction. Back into her nose went the tubes, and into her arms the intravenous needles.

"Will she have to be operated on again?" I inquired anxiously of the surgeon. "What caused the blockage? How long will she be hospitalized this time?"

"Only one Person knows all the answers," replied the physician, "and He isn't telling me. Whenever I try to outguess Him, He always proves me wrong."

"I have the same experience, doctor," I bemoaned.

Fortunately, additional surgery was avoided, and after about a week, our daughter was home again and on her way to full recovery. Later, in recalling the events connected with Bonnie's illness, I could clearly trace the guiding hand of God delivering her out of all her afflictions.

One bright note in the midst of the emotional suffering related to our daughter's maladies still brings a smile whenever I remember it . . .

Our little five-year-old granddaughter was staying with us shortly after her mother's second hospitalization. We were recording some of her childish songs on our tape recorder. In order to include her ordinary conversation, I suggested we talk a bit. I asked her a question.

"Honey, how did you feel when your Mommy was gone to the hospital?"

"Oh I feel bad!" she exclaimed. "One day I cried for Mommy because she was in the hospital and I wanted her home."

"Did you pray for your mother?" I inquired.

"Yes," she replied, nodding her head vigorously.

"Did Jesus answer your prayers?"

"One night He did," she said. "But one night I prayed and

prayed and He didn't—He didn't answer my prayers. So one night I prayed again—louder—and God heard me, and He did what He could. Then the next night He did it all. He made Mommy better."

How much wiser she was at five years of age regarding God's way of doing things—His timing particularly—than many adults are who presumptuously pray for an instant miracle in every illness. They demand that God overturn all natural and physical laws of healing just for their benefit.

Some of them justify this demand for an instantaneous miracle on the basis that it is always God's will to heal. They quote Scriptures such as: "Ask what you will, and it shall be done"; "Nothing is impossible with God"; "If you ask anything of God in faith believing, it shall be done"; "They shall lay hands on the sick, and they shall recover." And they assume that means right now, immediately.

If you are one who tends to agree with this type of spiritual behavior, let me ask you an important question. Why is it that you do not demand instant healing of your mental, moral, and spiritual character? Immediate perfection. Personal holiness. That is God's will too. Why is it that you do not pray to be made instantly whole spiritually?

"Oh, but that takes time," someone objects.

So does physical healing, as a general rule. This doesn't mean that God does not sometimes heal miraculously and instantaneously. He does. I have seen this happen, and have listened to the testimonies and documentary evidence of hundreds of people who have been divinely healed in this manner. But in all of these cases, I have carefully noted, the conditions were beyond natural or medical help. God did what He could—and what *only* He could do.

Just because we are not healed immediately does not mean that God hasn't heard us, or that He is not answering our prayer. He may not heal us our way and according to our timing. God is sovereign, and He does as He pleases. He answers our prayers His way, according to His timetable.

And that is a great deal better in the long run.

What About Us Who Are Not Healed?

The entire matter of God's timing as the Holy Spirit works in our lives is of crucial importance. For us to be changed into the image of Christ by the Spirit of the Lord, takes time. It is from glory to glory. Creation itself took time; so does re-creation. It takes time to get sick; it takes time to get well.

Maturity of character is built experience by experience, action upon reaction, test upon test. Of necessity, this involves a process, and a process takes time. We are not miraculously conformed to Christlikeness at conversion, nor by the Baptism in the Holy Spirit. We are not made complete and perfect by graduating from Bible school, or by becoming a minister or a missionary. We ourselves must undergo a gradual work of transformation and maturity.

What has this got to do with healing? Everything. It is inseparably bound up with it.

Since God's purpose for His children is essentially spiritual, our prayers for physical healing are only "fringe benefit" prayers. As such, they are answered according to the central purpose. And bodily healing is not that central purpose.

If God heals some sinner instantaneously, it is because the physical plane is the only approach He has to that person. Through the flesh, He seeks to reach the soul. A saved child of God already functions in the realm of the Spirit, and God deals with him differently. "For God dealeth with you as with sons; for what son is there whom his father chasteneth not?" And the reason God disciplines His sons is "that we may be partakers of his holiness" (Heb. 12:7,10ASV).

Never forget that if we are completely whole, we are fully developed in mental and moral character, and our spiritual character is sinless, pure, and holy. That kind of wholeness is not injected into us. Even the Great Physician cannot give us a shot of "instant holiness." We have to desire it, seek it, follow after it, yield our will and our ways to Him, and let Him work in us to bring it about.

"Well, Carmen," said my heavenly Teacher, breaking into my musing, "this is a decided change from your complaint-reaction

82

to physical affliction in the past. How are you reacting to the business troubles?"

"I've got a singing feeling now, Lord, instead of a sinking one as I drive up in front of the store," I told Him happily. "My tune hasn't changed, but the words have. I used to sing only this verse of a certain song, because that was what I identified with: 'I do not know, O Lord, why it should be Thy will for me to bear so much of heartache and of pain; I do not know, O Lord, why it should be Thy will for me to suffer loss when I have prayed for gain . . . ' That's what I used to sing."

"Yes," said the Spirit, "that was a familiar refrain of yours."

"Now I sing the chorus, because that's the part that really says it: 'But I do know Thou wilt not let me go; Thy way is always best, no matter what the test. And I do know if I but trust in Thee, all the darkness soon will pass, and I shall see.'

"Lord, I'm learning the truth of those words. I know that You are keeping me day by day. I'm learning the lesson of trust. 'Blessed is the man that trusts in the Lord,' as my little sign says. Anyone can blithely repeat 'trust in the Lord' Scripture verses. Even our coins bear the words, 'In God we trust.' But to actually trust in God in the face of an onslaught of adverse circumstances is quite a different thing. To make those verses and that inscription a reality in the daily life—to literally subsist by trust—is not so easy."

My Companion made no reply, so I continued. "I used to take for granted that we would have an adequate income from our store, and that someone would be there to do the work if we got sick. But now I'm finding out that nothing can be taken for granted. 'Give us our daily bread, our daily health and strength. Deliver us from evil.' That's what I pray now."

"Those truths have been a part of the Scripture for a long time," observed the Spirit.

"Yes," I agreed, "but now those truths are a part of me!"

"Then I would say that you have added trust to your faith," said my Teacher.

"That's because You—who gave me faith in the first place— have added trust to that faith," I asserted gratefully. "Annie

Johnson Flint's poem says it so well: 'He giveth more grace when the burdens grow greater; He sendeth more strength when the labors increase. To added affliction, He addeth His mercy; to multiplied trials, His multiplied peace.' "

"By the way, Lord," I commented, "the woman who penned those lines was one of 'us who are not healed.' She spent over forty years in a wheelchair. Yet she wrote those beautiful words: 'His love has no limit; His grace has no measure; His power has no boundary known unto men . . . ' "

" 'For out of His infinite riches in Jesus, He giveth, and giveth, and giveth again!' " quoted the Spirit, finishing the sentence. Then He said, "Carmen, we have had—in poetry and in your life—addition and multiplication. What we need now is subtraction. Some things need to be subtracted."

"From me?" I inquired uncomfortably.

"Yes, from you."

"Well, just so we don't have any division," I told Him. "Never divide Yourself from me, Lord. I couldn't bear it without You!"

"Division is not one of the works of the Spirit," He said.

"No, that's one of the works of the flesh," I replied. "But instead of subtracting, wouldn't it be easier just to do some erasing?"

"God has already erased your sins. To erase the works of the flesh from your character is another matter. I prefer to subtract you from the flesh, not to erase you from it."

"Remember when I wanted You to *extract* me from the flesh, Lord? I thought death was the way."

"Christ is the way."

This time it was I who finished the sentence: "And the truth, and the life."

XI

"They That Are Whole Have No Need of the Physician"

(Mark 2:17)

I sang many years ago in Sunday school, "Jesus wants
  me for a sunbeam, to shine for Him each day."
The Spirit said many years later in life's school, "I want
  you for sonship, to light for others the way."
The Bible said, "They that be wise shall shine as the
  brightness of the firmament; and they that turn many
  to righteousness as the stars for ever and ever." (Dan.
  12:3).

Early one morning, about five o'clock, the Holy Spirit awoke
me with these words:

"Carmen, today we are going to have an examination. I know
that you had anticipated writing about your saints, as you call
them; and also that you are eager to write up the interview you
had with one of the present-day saints. But for this chapter, I
have other plans."

I said nothing. He knew He had my consent, and I knew that
He was in full charge of what was to come forth.

"In some respects, this too might be termed an interview, though it is fundamentally an examination. I want to record your ordinary conversation, much as you did your little grand-daughter's. Be as free and open as she was. I want your answers to be spontaneous—unstudied. Will you do that?"

"Yes, Lord."

"Some of the questions I ask may appear to have no connecting pattern. But I know where I am leading."

I nodded my head in compliance.

"First of all," said my Teacher, "why did you remember that particular Sunday school song about the sunbeam?"

"Because it was the only religious song I ever sang as a child. My parents were not church people. A Christian man and his wife had a Sunday school class in the auditorium of the local grammar school. Some of the neighborhood children came, and I among them. I don't recall whether we had to memorize that song, or whether some other reason caused it to lodge in my sub-conscious mind."

"Did you believe the words you sang?"

"About Jesus wanting . . . me?"

"Yes."

"Well, I—"

There was a pause. Then, seemingly in a different vein, the Spirit asked, "What were the first words I ever spoke to you as you knelt in prayer at the altar of your church?"

Without the least hesitation, I repeated them exactly as I had heard them several years ago. I could never forget those words, for they were inscribed in my soul:

"I will lead you in paths of righteousness, if you are willing." It was the "if you are willing" that was emphasized, and that lingered acutely in my memory.

My Teacher's questions continued. "What did I say to you one morning in another church at the close of a Bible class?"

I gasped. "Do You really want me to tell that, Lord?"

"I would not have asked you otherwise."

"Well, I should explain that I was very fond of that class, having attended it regularly for about five years. At the close of the last session before the Christmas vacation period, the teacher said, 'Carmen, will you dismiss the class with prayer?' At the very same moment, I distinctly heard Your voice, Lord, say to me: 'And then, Carmen, dismiss yourself from the class.' I was so startled I hardly knew what I was praying. I was really shook up inside. I remember I hurried home and fell on my knees and asked You directly if You had spoken that to me and if You meant that I was not to return to the class again."

"And what did I reply?"

"You confirmed it to me in prayer, and then You confirmed it in Your Word."

"Where in the Word?"

"In Luke 2:29. 'Now let thy servant depart in peace, according to thy word' " (AP).

"What did you deduce from that verse?"

"I gathered from it that You were telling me it was time for me to leave the particular place and level of spiritual instruction of that Bible class, and go on to something else. You told me You would be my Teacher. I promised that I would just as faithfully set aside the same two hours every Wednesday morning, and instead of spending it in the class with my friends, I would spend it at home in the Word with You."

"Why did you think I led you out of the Bible class?"

"I supposed it was because it had become too elementary for me. I had outgrown it."

Suddenly a disturbing thought occurred to me. "Wait a minute, Lord!" I exclaimed. "I'd better not write that answer. My readers will say 'Ah-ha! That shows she thought she knew more than the teacher. Talk about pride—she's really got it!' "

"Never mind about your readers," said the Holy Spirit sternly. "What happened after that?"

"You told me to write a gracious note of explanation to my teacher and express my appreciation to her for the many years of inspiration and insight into the Word she had given me."

"And after you did that?"

"I waited upon You for the next step. I had no idea what You had in mind. You seemed to be silent. It was not until the very next Wednesday morning just before the time that the class would ordinarily begin that I received Your answer."

"How was that answer communicated?"

"By the radio. I was making the bed and listening to a Bible class broadcast over a Christian radio station. The teacher had just begun a series of lessons on the epistles of Peter. He read the words, 'Elect, according to the foreknowledge of God the Father, through sanctification of the Spirit, unto obedience and sprinkling of the blood of Jesus Christ' (I Pet. 1:2). I never heard another word after that. A bolt of heavenly lightning struck me. I moved like a robot to turn off the radio, and I fell on my face before You."

"And then what?" asked the Spirit.

"Those words—'the sprinkling of the blood'—burned clear through me, and they rang in my brain like carillon chimes in a bell tower."

"What did they mean to you?"

"They meant that was to be our lesson. That was where You were leading me—to a study of the blood of sprinkling. I knew there was a difference between the shed blood and the sprinkled blood. The latter was to be the subject of our private Bible class."

"What did you do next?"

"That morning I studied every Scripture in the Bible about the blood of sprinkling. I took notes, and what I learned caused me to walk around afterward in a daze. A wondrous daze, I must say."

"Were there any other words that kept recurring as you pondered the meaning of the Scripture from I Peter?"

"Yes—'sanctification.' "

"How would you distinguish between sanctification and salvation?" asked my Teacher.

"Salvation," I replied, "is a marvelous word that includes everything in the Gospel, even to the future redemption of the body. Sanctification is a part of salvation that is connected with the blood of Christ. But not so much the blood that was shed on Calvary for the remission of sins. Sanctification has more to do with the blood of Christ that He took with Him when He entered into the Holy of Holies in the temple in heaven."

"Did any of the other words in that Scripture impress you—'elect' and 'obedience,' for instance?"

"No, not then. I was too busy reeling around trying to absorb the full meaning of sanctification."

"Carmen, let me ask you another question. When you pray, what is the deepest cry of your spirit?"

A throatful of tears choked me as I gave Him the answer—for it was the answer that He Himself had been praying through me for many years. "I want to be holy. I want to be pure. Like You, Lord. Like You."

"And what are the words of the song you often sing when just you and I are together?"

I could only whisper them now . . . "Oh how I love my blessed Saviour, blessed Redeemer of my soul! Oh how I'm longing to be like Him—holy, and sinless, and pure."

For several moments, neither of us said anything. Then He spoke so sweetly, so gently: "Do you see now where I am leading you?"

"Yes, Lord," I replied. "But I am so far from—"

"I know," He broke in. "That's why I am here. I am near to the blood-sprinkled mercy seat in heaven, and I am near to the blood-sprinkled child on earth."

After He said that, for a little while I cried.

Again there was a period of silence. Then I ventured to ask, "Lord, we aren't going to go any farther, are we?"

" 'Yea, farther,' " He said. " 'Though a wise man think to know it, yet shall he not be able to find it.' "

"That must be a verse of Scripture You've just quoted," I remarked. "Where is it?"

"Look it up."

I did, and found it in Ecclesiastes 8:17. I read what preceded the words "yea farther." It was this: "Then I beheld all the work of God, that a man cannot find out the work that is done under the sun; because though a man labour to seek it out, yet he shall not find it; yea farther; though a wise man think to know it, yet shall he not be able to find it."

Strange words . . .

The Living Bible paraphrase made them clearer: "In my search for wisdom I observed all that was going on everywhere across the earth—ceaseless activity, day and night. (Of course, only God can see everything, and even the wisest man who says he knows everything, doesn't!)"

"In other words," I reflected, "no matter how high a person's IQ, or how great his spiritual advancement, or how exalted his opinion of himself, or the esteem in which he is held by others— there are many things man will never find out or know here. These are the mysteries of God that are beyond even the wisest person on earth."

Replied my Teacher, "What the wisest man cannot learn or find out, the Spirit can reveal. He who is truly wise seeks to know God, rather than the mysteries or pleasures of His creation."

"Lord," I said after a few moments of deliberation, "I do want to be wise—not in the eyes of men, but wise in the things of God."

"What did Daniel say about the wise?"

"He said that they will shine as brightly as the sun."

"And what did he say about those who turn many to righteousness?"

"They will shine as the stars in the heaven, forever."

"Do you know yet why I caused you to remember that little Sunday school song about the sunbeam?"

"Was it You who caused me to remember it?" I exclaimed in surprise. "Lord, did You know me way back then—when I was just a child?"

"Those whom God calls, He also foreknew."

I shook my head in amazement. "I guess Jesus really and truly wanted me to be a sunbeam, to shine for Him each day," I murmured.

"Now that you are no longer a child," said the Holy Spirit, "I want to shine forth from you in your daily life. I want to make you whole. Carmen, I have still another question to ask you."

"What is it, Lord?"

"In your present Sunday school, what did your teacher say in a recent lesson that caused you to utter two loud 'Amens' in class? Later you asked him over the telephone to repeat his statements."

"I have them right here, Lord. He couldn't recall exactly what he said. He mentioned that You had revealed it to him only that week. But he obtained the tape from a woman in the class, typed out that section, and brought it to me. This is it:

" 'God wants to present Himself to the world through you. He is more anxious to present Himself through you than He is about your bodily comfort. Whatever it takes that the world might see Christ in you, God is more concerned about that than He is about healing your body.

" 'Because we get a little pain and discomfort in the body, we want Him to set aside all that He wants to do, just to make us comfortable. We make the mistake of thinking that the only way we can be comfortable and happy in this world is through a sound and healthy body. The truth of the matter is that the only way we can have peace and comfort in this world is through the presence of God, regardless of the condition of the natural body! As long as there isn't anything that separates us from God, we can have peace in Him.' "

Departing a moment from the reading of the typewritten words, I remarked to the Holy Spirit that this is where I said my first loud "Amen." Then I resumed reading the transcript.

" 'The loss of natural things is not always enough to bring us to godly sorrow that worketh repentance. Sometimes it takes bodily affliction to bring this about. Happy is the person who doesn't need this kind of dealing from a kind and loving heavenly Father. But if this is necessary to fulfill the plan and purpose of God, He will pour out the grace necessary to get the job done.

" 'Remember that God's primary purpose in all His dealings with us is to first save our immortal soul, and then to restore us to fellowship with Him. He also wants to save others by revealing Himself through us to them. We must be willing, as Paul said, 'to suffer all things that Christ might be seen' in every walk of life and every circumstance and environment.' "

When I finished reading these words, I said, "That's what caused me to give vent to my second loud 'Amen' in class."

I told the Lord, "I am so fortunate to have a man of spiritual wisdom and maturity to be my Sunday school teacher. He has taught me much."

"It is to those who, by teaching, make others wise that the Scripture from Daniel (12:3) refers," the Spirit informed me. "The original wording of the phrase 'they that be wise' makes this clear."

The Amplified Bible provided further confirmation. It read: "And the *teachers* . . . shall shine . . . and those who turn many to...uprightness and right standing with God shall *give forth light* like the stars for ever."

"Those who turn others to righteousness shall give forth light," emphasized the heavenly Teacher, "Do you see now why I said I wanted you for sonship, to light for others the way?"

Overcome with the picture of His purpose for my life, as He had put the pieces together, I could only review the scenes that had been brought into focus . . .

From a sunbeam . . . down paths of righteousness . . . because of a blood-sprinkled mercy seat in heaven . . . through service to the living God . . . to the holy, pure, sinless image of Christ.

I fell on my knees. "Lord, these things are too wonderful for me! I am not wise enough to teach others, to turn others to righteousness. I, myself, am still learning—am still unrighteous."

"Carmen, some things you have already learned, and these are to be passed on to others. You have learned from your physical afflictions, you have learned from your business troubles; you learned from your critics, from your teachers, your physician, your granddaughter. You learned from life itself. You learned from the dictionary, from spiritual books, and from the sacred Scriptures. And now I will tell you something more."

"What is that, Lord?" I asked, a bit wary of what to expect.

"Many people are going to learn from you."

For a moment I was speechless. Then, still kneeling, I bowed my face to the floor. "Lord," I whispered, "if they learn anything from me, it will have come from You. It will be a gift from You . . . to me . . . and through me."

"Every good gift and every perfect gift is from above," said the Spirit, "and cometh down from the Father of lights, with whom there is no variableness, neither shadow that is cast by the turning" (James 1:17AP).

To this, I could only say another "Amen," a quiet one.

XII
"Make...an Oil of Holy Ointment"

(Exod. 30:25)

The dictionary said, "A saint is a holy or godly person; especially one regenerated and sanctified, or undergoing sanctification."

The Bible said, "Those who are sanctified in Christ Jesus are called to be saints" (I Cor. 1:2 AP).

One of the chief saints said, "Christ Jesus came into the world to save sinners; of whom I am chief" (I Tim. 1:15).

"Carmen, you may choose the subject for our writing today," the voice of my Teacher sounded in my spiritual ears just as I was awaking.

"Lord, You know what I will choose. I will choose to write about my saints," I immediately replied.

"Very well," He said. "You have studied the lives and writings of many of them, and taken copious notes of the things you wanted to remember. Draw from those hoarded resources and pass around some of the choice pieces."

94

"Like the chocolates, Lord?" I asked Him, referring to a time a few years ago when the Holy Spirit gave me what might be called a "flash vision." It happened as I was sitting at home alone, engrossed in my favorite pastime, studying the Word of God. He had been opening the eyes of my understanding and flooding my mind with an abundance of rich insights. Suddenly He drew the curtain, and all I could see in front of me was a box of See's chocolates. Then I saw myself eating them, the whole box!

"What's the meaning of this, Lord?" I asked in bewilderment.

"You are doing with the Word of God what you just saw yourself do with that box of chocolates," He answered. "Eating all of it, and sharing none."

"What do You expect me to do, Lord?"

"Pass the chocolates around."

That very night I tried to obey Him by giving a brief testimony at church containing some of the select truths that He had imparted to me. They were well received. A couple of weeks later, I spoke at the midweek Bible class; and though I again passed on several very choice Scriptures, this time something went wrong.

The next morning I asked the Holy Spirit about it. "What was the trouble, Lord? I was just trying to follow Your instructions."

"I think some vinegar got into those chocolates last night," He stated flatly.

My face flushed with embarrassment. I remembered that I had used the Word of God, in what I thought was instruction in righteousness, to correct a Christian brother. But now the Holy Spirit lost no time in correcting me. This is what He said:

"Give the instruction you see, and leave the correction to Me."

He has since caused me to understand that unless I am motivated solely by the inspiration of the Word, without any desire to reprove somebody else, and unless I speak the truth in love—some vinegar is very apt to spill into the chocolates. And it is the vinegar, not the candy, that the listeners will get. They will taste my spirit rather than my words.

"I don't see how any vinegar can get into a box of chocolates taken from the lives of my saints," I told my Teacher.

"Did you have no thought at all of using these saints to re-prove any of your Christian brethren, Carmen?" He asked probingly.

Again I was abashed, for in His discernment of my motives, He must have gotten a whiff of vinegar. But only a whiff. I did want to show those people who insist that it is God's will to heal all believers that there have been many exemplary lives—famous saints—who have not been healed. Indeed, some have suffered terribly most of their days. These illustrious saints certainly refute the teaching that if a Christian is not healed, it is due to unbelief, disobedience, or sin. The merest glance at their consecrated lives should eliminate that kind of dogmatism.

"That was the least of the reasons I had in the back of my mind for choosing to write about my saints," I protested to my Teacher. "Their lives were so much more than the suffering they endured. The beauty of their holiness is what I really want to bring out."

"When you do," He cautioned, "remember two things. First and foremost, you cannot make another person into a saint. You can tell Stevie to do what Mommy says, to quote your little granddaughter. But you cannot change your brother. Only the Spirit of God can do that."

"And even You have a difficult enough time, Lord!" I de-clared. "What was the other thing You wanted me to remem-ber?"

"Keep the lid tightly closed on the vinegar bottle."

My next remark returned to the subject at hand. "These saints are shining examples of many of the things we have been talking about."

"Literally, *shining* examples," agreed the Spirit. "In them, the light of God clearly shone."

"Oh yes!" I exclaimed rapturously. "I know that the light of the world is Jesus, and the Bible is a daily light unto my path. But these saints have reflected some lovely beams of light to me, and I want to select a few and pass them on to others. Besides, Lord," I added defensively, "it's much better than going any farther into my own life."

"Your life is an example too," He stated.

"Of what?" I inquired. "Of 'don't let this happen to you'?"

Ignoring my witticism, He replied, "You yourself are known and read by all men, whether they read your books or not."

Stricken by the knowledge of what a poor example I am, fervently I implored, "Then please, dear Lord, write on me! Write Your laws deep in my heart. Make me readable in Your sight. And in the eyes of men, let me be an example of Christ's handwriting—with all my mistakes blotted out."

"So be it," responded the Spirit. "For now, you may go ahead and write about your saints. You have perfect liberty to tell the things that impress you most about their lives."

At first I thought, "Oh great! I'm on my own now. I'm free to write what I please in this chapter!"

But it wasn't long before a shock wave hit me. I didn't really *want* to do just as I pleased. I didn't even want to be "on my own." I honestly wanted to do what He would have me do—to have Him guide me—companion me—correct me—the way things had been before.

"Don't leave me, Lord, just because You've given me free rein!" I besought Him.

He made no reply. His presence was not removed, just standing to one side.

Two of my saints were members of a monastic order, and two of them led ordinary lives outside of any religious organization. I decided to begin with St. Teresa, since she was the first to have a direct influence on my spiritual life.

St. Teresa of Avila was a Spanish nun who lived in the sixteenth century. Born in March of 1515, she died in an Augustinian monastery at the age of sixty-seven. But oh, the in-between! What a life of piety, humility, discipline, wisdom and service!

She was eighteen years old when she left her father's house to enter a convent. The night before her departure, she attended a party and danced with several young caballeros. They were captivated by her great beauty. One of them said, "Señorita, you have very beautiful eyes."

Teresa, thinking of the cloistered way that lay ahead, replied, "Take a good long look, Señor. This is the last time you will ever see them."

From the beginning, she was happy in the religious life. But soon illness struck, and she was forced to return home. During the period of her recovery, she resolved to become a nun.

"When I took the habit," she later wrote, "our Lord at once made me understand how He helps those who deny themselves in order to serve Him." The joy she felt then never left her. All the days of her life she was betrothed unto the Lord.

Bodily affliction never left her either. Her health worsened, leaving her heart seriously impaired. Along with many other ailments, she was a victim of consumption. Still in her early twenties, she found her strength was gone, and her pain intensified. She could take only liquids; a fever burned unabatedly, and her limbs began to shrink. She was given up by the physicians.

For three months she lingered like this. All the while, her conversation was with God. She was encouraged by the words of Job: "Shall we receive good at the hand of God, and shall we not receive evil?" (Job 2:10).

After four days of unconsciousness, last sacraments were administered. Funeral solemnities were performed, and her grave lay open waiting for her body.

But she regained consciousness.

Her tongue was bitten to pieces. There was a choking in her throat because she had taken nothing—not even water. All her bones seemed to be out of joint, and the disorder in her head was extreme. She was bent together like a coil of ropes, and was able to move only one finger of her right hand.

Managing somehow to speak, she begged that she be allowed to go into the chapel for confession. So bruised was she, she could not bear to be touched. Pains were sharp and constant. Cold fits alternated with the fever, and nausea swept over her. They took her into the chapel in a sheet.

From that moment on, she commenced to improve—though for three years she was paralyzed. Then she began to crawl on her hands and knees—praising God.

"I am resigned to the will of God," she said, "even if He leaves me in this state forever." Those around her marveled at her patience, for if it had not come from God, she could never have endured so great an affliction with such joy.

"When I saw how helpless I was through paralysis," she wrote, "and still so young, and how the physicians of the world had dealt with me, I determined to ask those of heaven to heal me."

Solely through prayer and supplication, she—a paralytic—was raised up, when everyone wondered how she could even be alive. "The Lord gives us desires and resolutions," she explained, "then tests them by experience, helping us to succeed therein."

Notwithstanding the miraculous healing of her paralysis, Teresa continued to suffer physically in other ways until the end of her earthly journey. This did not stop her from living a life of prayer, contemplation, and active service for others.

She is well-known for her reformation work within the Carmelite order, and for her founding and organizing of many convents. She wrote a number of books. Self-taught, and taught by the Holy Spirit, she possessed an intellectual clarity and a depth of spiritual wisdom that astounds all who read her writings.

Teresa saw the value of learning joined to holiness, and in her, both were united. "Do not foster the cult of holy stupidity," she told her Sisters; and most of her books were written so that they would have ample instruction in the ways of God. For her holy life, she was canonized forty years after her death. Four hundred years later, in recognition of her written works, she was declared one of the two women Doctors of the Roman Catholic Church.

Endowed with the light and fire of the Holy Ghost, and immersed in the love of Christ, Teresa abandoned herself completely into the hands of God. Her soul, magnificently reflecting His grace and His glory, was willingly lost in Him.

"I know by experience," she wrote in mid-life, "the only way not to fall is to cling to the cross, and put our trust in Him who was nailed thereto."

During her lifetime, she was the recipient of communications with God which have made her a classic mystic. She experienced many supernatural visitations by the Lord Jesus Christ, for Whom she had a deep and intimate love. "All my gain," she said, "has come through revelations and raptures, in which I am no more than the canvas a picture is painted on." To her, Jesus was more directly present as a known and loved person than any of those with whom she was in daily contact.

Mystic though she was, she was nevertheless a woman of compelling charm—affectionate and motherly. She was also full of wit and practicality. Salted through her books of profound spiritual doctrine is her irrepressible wit and her many humorous comments, particularly regarding the foibles and funny ways of her fellow human beings.

She had her own idea of what a saint should be like, and her most caustic remarks were directed toward those who felt that to be holy meant to be gloomy. "God save us from sad-faced saints," she used to say; and she strictly forbade the superiors of her convents to accept "melancholy" individuals.

"Lord knows," she told them, "this life is hard enough without having people like that around."

She met with many obstacles in her life, and was criticized on every hand by clerics and prelates. But her consecration and her determination won out in the end, and her work succeeded.

From the abundance of St. Teresa's spiritual instruction, I have selected the following comments to pass on:

"What difficulties and what terrors Satan troubles them with who would draw near to God! . . . I passed nearly twenty years falling and rising. I had no sweetness in God, and no pleasure in the world. During twenty-eight years of prayer, I spent more than eighteen in that strife and contention which arose out of my attempts to reconcile God and the world. As to the other ten, in them the grounds of the warfare were changed. Inasmuch as I was serving God, and aware of the vanity of the world, all has been pleasant."

"I had many friends to help me to fall; but as to rising again, I was so much left to myself that I wonder now I was not always on the ground! I praise God for His mercy; for it was He only who stretched out His hand to me."

"Our Lord Jesus is He by whom all good things come."

"If we deny ourselves, little by little we shall eventually reach that height which many saints by His grace have reached. If they had never resolved to desire, and had never little by little acted upon that resolve, they never could have ascended to so high a state."

"Why does a soul in a state of grace receive so much more than one not in a state of grace? The difference does not lie with God. Is it the fault of the sun that it does not illumine a lump of pitch when its rays strike it, as it illumines a globe of crystal?"

"Our Lord once said to me: 'Let no one think that of himself he can abide in the light, any more than he can hinder the natural night from coming on. That depends on My grace. The best means he can have for retaining the light is the conviction in his soul that he can do nothing of himself, and that it comes from Me. Even if he were in the light, the instant I withdraw, night will come.' "

"In the eyes of Infinite Wisdom, believe me, a little striving after humility, and a single act thereof, are worth more than all the science in the world. . . . I have seen, within myself, how mean a soul can be if God is not always working in it."

"Though it is painful to see ourselves as we are, yet true humility does not disturb the soul. On the contrary, it consoles. It brings calm, sweetness, and light. It is painful, yes; but we see how great is the mercy of our Lord in allowing the soul to grieve over its offenses against God."

"Let us labor to consider the virtues and the good qualities which we discern in others; and with our own great sins cover our eyes, so that we may see none of their failings."

"Many of the Lord's words to me are reproaches, and He sends them when I fall into imperfections. They correct me. Others bring my former sins into remembrance—particularly when He is about to bestow upon me some special grace. Some are warnings against certain dangers to myself or others. Many are prophecies of future things—given three or four years beforehand. All have been fulfilled."

"Strong souls are chosen by our Lord to do good to others— still their strength is not their own."

"My soul is a garden, and our Lord walks in it. I beseech Him to increase the fragrance of the little flowers of virtues which are beginning to bud—and preserve them, that they might be to His glory. Cut those He likes, because I know they will grow the better."

"Perfection is a thing of growth, and of laboring after freedom from the cobwebs of memory. This requires time. . . . He who does not cease to walk and to press onwards, arrives at last—even if late."

"In true prayer, the whole soul is occupied in loving Him whom the understanding has toiled to know. It loves what it has not comprehended, and rejoices because it has lost itself in order to gain itself the more."

"For those who persevere in prayer, if they take a little trouble, God gives sweetness, in order that, by the help it supplies, they may bear their trials. . . . One drop of water from the kingdom that shall never end, if the soul but tastes it, renders the things of this world utterly loathsome."

"One day, wondering whether it would not be better for me if I occupied myself always with prayer, I heard this: 'During this life, the true gain consists not in striving after greater joy in Me, but in doing My will. I think more of obedience than penance.' "

"I see that Christ's life was one of suffering, and I ask Him to send that to me, giving me first the grace to bear it. . . . Our Lord said to me that there is no obedience where there is no resolution to suffer; that I was to think of His sufferings, and then everything would be easy."

"It is possible for the soul to be purified by pain—burnished, or refined as gold in the crucible, so that it might be the better enamelled with His gifts, and the dross burnt away in this life."

"Once after Communion, our Lord Jesus Christ appeared to

me in a vision, as He is wont to do. I saw that He had on His head—instead of a crown of thorns—a crown of great splendor over the part where the wounds of that crown must have been. I began to be sorrowful to think how great the pain must have been because of the many wounds. Our Lord told me not to be sad because of those wounds, but for the many wounds which men inflict upon Him now."

"On another occasion, Our Lord said to me: 'Believe Me, My daughter, his trials are the heaviest whom My Father loves most; trials are the measure of His love. . . . Behold My wounds. My will is that My blood should profit thee. I shed it in much suffering, and as thou seest, thou has the fruition of it in great joy.' "

Teresa closed the last letter she ever wrote by saying:

"O that I could clearly explain the peace and quiet my soul has found! Everything in me is directed to the honor of God, to the doing of His will more and more, and the advancement of His glory. My likings and my dislikings have little power to take from me His presence. This is always the state I am in, except when my great infirmities oppress me.

"Sometimes God has me suffer without any inward comfort, but my will never swerves from the will of God. I long to see His face. Yet I wish to live—if such be His good pleasure—to serve Him still longer. And if I might help by my prayers to make but one soul love and praise Him more, I think that of more importance than to dwell in glory."

The letter was signed by the name she always chose to be called—not "St. Teresa of Avila," as she is known in religious and secular history books, but simply "Teresa of Jesus."

Her words on her deathbed were, "Lord, now we shall soon see one another. . . . " But St. Teresa had long since seen her Lord.

XIII
"I Will Restore Health Unto Thee"

(Jer. 30:17)

Carlyle said, "Music . . . is the speech of angels."

Matthew Arnold said, "Poetry . . . is the most beautiful, impressive, and widely effective mode of saying things."

My hymn book said, "Musicians and poets, the saints and the redeemed . . . all have seen the hunger in the heart unsatisfied except through song."

As I meditated on the wisdom revealed in the words of St. Teresa, and the purity of her life, suddenly I stopped short.

Holy and wise though she was, and the recipient of so many gifts from Christ, nonetheless, one of God's most marvelous gifts was not hers—the gift of song. Poetry set to music makes song. When the Gospel of the Lord Jesus Christ is put into poetry adaptable for a musical setting, then we have a most glorious gift of the Holy Spirit.

Such a gift was bestowed upon the second of my saints—Frances Jane Crosby, more familiarly known as Fanny Crosby.

From her heart and soul poured forth poetry that beautifully and impressively expressed the Gospel. And when others set her poems to music, they were indeed a widely effective mode of saying things.

Something else brought me up short in my reflections. St. Teresa was not the first saint to influence my spiritual life. Fanny Crosby was. For it was her words clothed in music that spoke to me long before I ever heard of St. Teresa. When I was a teenage girl, those words found lodgment in my mind, and their message remained in my soul during all my wanderings toward God.

"Pass me not, O gentle Savior, hear my humble cry; while on others Thou art calling, do not pass me by. . . . " Who has sung that gospel song and not been moved in the heart? I know that I was. And it moves me yet every time I hear it.

"Tell me the story of Jesus, write on my heart every word; tell me the story most precious, sweetest that ever was heard. . . . " Few have told that story more sweetly than the woman who wrote those words.

"Redeemed—how I love to proclaim it! Redeemed by the blood of the Lamb; redeemed through His infinite mercy, His child, and forever I am." And His child she was, through all the days of her ninety-five years on this earth.

Born in New York in March of 1820, Fanny Crosby was blind from infancy. Negligence on the part of a doctor caused her to lose her sight at the age of six weeks. Her physical sight was totally gone; but with the eyes of her spirit, she clearly saw Him who is invisible to the natural sight of all of us.

"Someday, when fades the golden sun beneath the rosy-tinted west . . . " she wrote in one of her poems. How could she who never saw a sunset describe it as a golden sun that faded into a rosy-tinted west? Never to have beheld the beauty of color— what a loss! But some with two good eyes have never beheld the beauty of Jesus—and how much greater is that loss!

Those words about the golden sun and the rose-tinted west are found in the one poem Fanny was reluctant to have set to music. She liked to use this poem when she addressed meetings, and no doubt felt that if it became well-known, it would be less desirable for her individual use, The name of the poem is "Saved by Grace."

"Someday the silver cord will break, and I no more as now shall sing; but O, the joy when I shall wake within the palace of the King! . . . And I shall see Him face to face, and tell the story—Saved by grace."

Fanny Crosby was educated at the New York School for the Blind. After graduation, she taught for eleven years in the same school. When she was thirty-eight years old, she married one of her pupils—a musician who was also blind. Two years later, her poems were first set to music, though she had attained much fame as a poet and writer during her early years.

Her first nationally successful song was one that I would like to have sung at my funeral. Many a night I drift off to sleep mentally singing its opening words, which are also the title of the poem: "Safe in the arms of Jesus, safe on His gentle breast. There by His love o'ershaded, sweetly my soul shall rest." And when I fall asleep for the last time, I pray that it will be in the arms of Jesus.

Fanny Crosby was a prolific writer. Over eight thousand of her song-poems have been published, of which about sixty are still in use. She never composed without a New Testament held open before her sightless eyes. The texts supplied by this blind saint have profoundly influenced and greatly strengthened the field of gospel music.

"Jesus, keep me near the cross, there a precious fountain, free to all—a healing stream, flows from Calvary's mountain. In the cross, in the cross, be my glory ever; till my raptured soul shall find rest beyond the river."

"All the way my Savior leads me; what have I to ask beside? Can I doubt His tender mercy, Who through life has been my Guide?" . . . "He hideth my soul in the cleft of the rock that shadows a dry, thirsty land; He hideth my life in the depths of His love, and covers me there with His hand."

"Though your sins be as scarlet, they shall be as white as snow; though they be red like crimson, they shall be as wool. Hear the voice that entreats you, 'O return ye unto God.' He is of great compassion and abundant love. 'Look unto Me, ye people,' saith the Lord your God. He'll forgive your transgressions, and remember them no more."

One day a well-known writer of music and verse played a melody for Fanny Crosby on the piano and asked, "Fanny, what does that tune say to you?"

The reply came after a few moment's thought—"Blessed assurance, Jesus is mine!" And within minutes, the famous song was completed . . . "Oh, what a foretaste of glory divine! Heir of salvation, purchase of God, born of His Spirit, washed in His blood."

The beauty of Fanny Crosby's life is best glimpsed in the glorious words that flowed from her inspired pen. I love to bathe my soul in that river . . .

"Savior, more than life to me, I am clinging close to Thee; let Thy precious blood applied, keep me ever near Thy side. Every day, every hour, let me feel Thy cleansing power; may Thy tender love to me bind me closer, closer, Lord, to Thee."

"Praise Him! praise Him! Jesus, our blessed Redeemer! Sing, O Earth, His wonderful love proclaim! Hail Him! Hail Him! highest archangels in glory; strength and honor give to His holy name!"

"To God be the glory, great things He hath done, so loved He the world that He gave us His Son, Who yielded His life an atonement for sin, and opened the Lifegate that all may go in."

"Jesus is tenderly calling thee home—calling today; why from the sunshine of love wilt thou roam farther and farther away? . . . Jesus is waiting; O come to Him now—waiting today; come with thy sins, at His feet lowly bow; come, and no longer delay."

"To the work! To the work! we are servants of God; let us follow the path that our Master has trod. . . . Toiling on, toiling on . . . let us hope, let us watch, and labor till the Master comes."

"Rescue the perishing, care for the dying, snatch them in pity from sin and the grave; weep o'er the erring one, lift up the fallen, tell them of Jesus the mighty to save."

"Holy, holy, holy is the Lord! Sing, O ye people, gladly adore Him; let the mountains tremble at His word, let the hills be joyful before Him."

"I am Thine, O Lord, I have heard Thy voice, and it told Thy love to me; but I long to rise in the arms of faith, and be closer drawn to Thee. Draw me nearer, blessed Lord, to the cross where Thou hast died; draw me nearer . . . to Thy precious, bleeding side."

"Close to Thee, close to Thee; all along my pilgrim journey, Savior, let me walk with Thee. . . . Gladly will I toil and suffer, only let me walk with Thee. . . . Lead me through the vale of shadows, bear me o'er life's fitful sea; then the gate of life eternal may I enter, Lord, with Thee."

With these lovely words—made lovelier still by melody—singing in my heart, I sat for a long time contemplating the wonder of a saint like Fanny Crosby.

If a person didn't know otherwise, he would never dream by reading her poems that she was physically afflicted in any way. There is not one note of complaint, self-pity, or discouragement. On the contrary, her words radiate joy, the uplift of implicit faith and trust in her Savior, the assurance of God's love and care.

While she wrote about "the healing stream that flows from Calvary's mountain," yet she herself was not healed. Why?

To give the stock reasons that many Christians give regarding a believer who fails to experience healing—not enough faith, sin in the life, demon oppression, some hidden mental, emotional or spiritual block—would be a gross insult to Fanny Crosby! As indeed it would be to St. Teresa, and the countless other great saints who were not healed.

"Why, Lord?" I asked Him. "Why didn't You touch the eyes of this blind saint and open them as You did when Jesus walked the earth? He said He was sent to bring 'recovery of sight to the blind,' among the many other blessings of His Spirit-anointed ministry. Is He not the same yesterday, today, and forever?"

"He does not change," replied the Spirit. "But His ministry

does."

"I don't understand, Lord."

"What answer did Jesus give to His disciples when they asked Him about the man who was born blind?"

"He told them that the cause of the blindness was not sin; but that the works of God would be made manifest in him."

"And they were manifest in him, regardless of the cause, were they not?" He queried.

"Yes," I replied. "Jesus healed the blind man by anointing his eyes with clay and sending him to wash in the pool of Siloam. He gave that man sight. Why didn't He heal Fanny Crosby?"

"Because He had a different purpose for her," declared the Spirit. "In His earthly ministry, Jesus opened many blind eyes. But in His heavenly ministry, He had something better for Fanny Crosby."

"Something better than the restoration of physical sight?" I exclaimed.

"Yes," He said. "He gave her spiritual sight to see only Him. That was the way the works of God were made manifest in her. Because she was blind, her eyes were closed to the things of this world from infancy. Remember your Saint Teresa said it took her eighteen years of prayer to become blind—blind to the vanity of this world!"

"I do remember that, Lord. And I know that spiritual blessings from God are much better gifts than physical ones. I remember the day You spoke to me under the hair dryer and asked me if there was something You could give me that was more important to me than healing."

"And you responded immediately that there was." Then He asked—so tenderly, "Have you ever regretted your answer, Carmen?"

"Never!" I avowed emphatically. "Never, Lord."

XIV
"If We Suffer, We Shall Also Reign"

(II Tim. 2:12)

David said, "Let my prayer be counted as incense before
thee, and the lifting up of my hands as an evening
sacrifice" (Ps. 141:2 RSV).

Paul said, "Christ loved us, and gave himself up for us, a
fragrant offering and sacrifice to God" (Eph. 5:2 RSV).

God said, "And the other lamb thou shalt offer at evening
...for a sweet savor unto the Lord" (Exod. 29:41 SCO).

My next saint is a man. He lived a long time ago, over three
hundred years before St. Teresa, and she lived over three
hundred years before Fanny Crosby. So this takes us back to the
end of the twelfth century.

It was a single sentence that this man spoke (or wrote) that
first intrigued me. For years it lingered in my mind, until finally I
made a study of his life. And what rich discoveries awaited me
there!

The sentence was this: "For it is in dying that we are born to eternal life." The man, of course, is St. Francis of Assisi, and those words conclude his famous prayer.

I used to think, "St. Francis, why did you say that? Dying does not gain a person birth into eternal life. The most familiar verse in all the Bible—John 3:16—plainly teaches that it is only whosoever believes in the only begotten Son of God that shall have everlasting life."

Jesus Himself declared, "This is life eternal, that they might know the only true God, and Jesus Christ whom He has sent" (John 17:3 AP). He further qualified this truth by saying, "Whoso eateth my flesh, and drinketh my blood, hath eternal life" (John 6:54). And in another place, speaking of His sheep, He said, "I give unto them eternal life" (John 10:28).

Later I came to understand why St. Francis said what he did about eternal life. His words are not in conflict with the Scriptures. It *is* in dying that we are born to eternal life—in dying to self, not in merely experiencing physical death. God has given eternal life, and that life is in His Son—nowhere else. When we are born again in Christ, we should begin the process of dying to the self-life in order that we might begin to live in Him.

In early manhood, Francis of Assisi had an encounter with the Lord Jesus which so drastically changed him that it caused sudden death to his old self. Most of us don't die to our self-seeking habit patterns so quickly, so thoroughly, nor so easily. Self, as a rule, dies a very hard, slow death—fighting every inch of the way.

Christians who refuse to die to self remain spiritual babies all their days. How such immature believers need to be healed spiritually! They have been saved, but not made whole. They came to Christ for salvation and received the forgiveness of sins that His shed blood provides. But the great benefit of the sprinkled blood has not been their experience. Why? Because self is still on the throne. The mind, heart, and will have never been submitted in obedience to the process of sanctification by the Holy Spirit. If a believer's desire to please self—which is the basic motivating factor of human nature—continues unchanged despite conver-

111

sion, that believer becomes a spiritual dwarf.

God's way of holiness is not as important to this type of believer as getting his own way. He is occupied with self, instead of being preoccupied with the Lord. He has no conception of what the crucified life means, no desire to find out, and no will to put forth any effort toward that end.

Francis was not one of these . . .

Disposing of his wealth, and turning his back on his former life, he forever thereafter devoted himself to the service of the poor and afflicted. The rule of the Franciscan Order which he founded was based on strict poverty. His followers existed by receiving alms, and were not allowed to own personal property.

Francis was not just dead to self. He was totally alive to God—and therein lies his sainthood.

He was born in 1182 and died in 1226. He lived only forty-four years; but when I read the full story of his bodily sufferings, I wonder that he lasted that long.

"From the beginning of my conversion, I was always infirm," Francis wrote. At the age of thirty-nine, his health worsened to such an extent that he was plunged into deep depression. He was a man much given to prayer, and though he prayed that the Lord would set him free from his tribulations, he was not relieved from his depression for two years.

One day in church he heard the words of Jesus spoken by an interior Voice: "If you have faith as a grain of mustard seed, you shall say to that mountain, 'Remove hence to another place,' and it shall remove."

Francis asked, "Lord, what is this mountain?"

Again the Voice spoke. "This mountain is your temptation."

Francis answered, "Lord, be it done to me as Thou hast said."

Immediately he was completely delivered of the depression, so that it seemed to him that he had never so much as had any. He was *not* restored to physical health. But the mountain of his temptation—that of letting physical affliction keep his faith under a dark cloud of despondency—had, indeed, been cast into the sea.

The sovereign cure for all depression, according to Francis, is spiritual joy. "The devil exults most when he can filch joy from one of God's servants," he said. "With joy present, Satan can do nothing. He cannot hurt Christ's servants when he sees them filled with holy mirth. Therefore, when we are troubled about anything, we should pray, and remain in our heavenly Father's presence until He restores the joy of our salvation. If we tarry in gloom, that Babylonian stuff will increase; and unless it is purged out, it will produce rust in the heart."

The thing that has always impressed me most about the life of this great saint is the fact that he was a stigmatic—one who bore in his own body the marks of the crucified Christ. Of course, he could never have received this ultimate seal of the Holy Spirit had he not prepared for it by living a crucified life himself.

The story surrounding the imprinting of the stigmata is, to me, most beautiful . . .

It happened two years before his death. Due to ill health, he had retired from active direction of his Order and had given himself completely to prayer. Long had he borne the stigmata in his heart. Now the hour was coming for the marks of Christ's wounds to be made visible in his flesh.

In the spring of 1224, Francis decided that he would spend the Lenten season at a certain mountain which had been given to him eleven years before. He had been there several times; this was the last time he was to go there. He took with him four chosen brothers.

On the last stage of the difficult ascent, they asked a peasant if he would lend his donkey to carry Francis, who was weary and ill. When he found that it was Francis, the peasant said to him, "Try then to be as good as people think you are!"

At this, Francis got off the donkey and kissed the man's feet in thanks for the admonition.

When they reached the summit of the mountain, they had a few days of rest before Lent began. One night as he lay on his bed on the bare rock—prior to sinking into the little sleep he permitted himself—Francis had a vision of an angel.

"I will play for you," said this shining one, "as we play before the throne of God." With that, the angel drew his bow across the string. But he made only a single stroke. Had he made another, Francis told the brothers the next morning, he could not have endured so ineffable a beauty, and his soul and body would have parted.

One month after Lent had begun, an angel appeared to Francis to forewarn him to more strictly prepare himself "humbly and with all patience to receive whatever God will give thee and work in thee."

Francis answered, "I am ready to endure with patience all things whatsoever my Lord will do unto me."

The next morning, before the break of dawn, Francis prayed, "O my Lord Jesus Christ, I pray Thee to grant me two graces before I die. The first is that I may feel in my soul and in my body, so far as this may be, the pangs Thou didst bear in the hour of Thy most bitter passion. . . . The second is that I may feel in my heart, so far as this may be, the exceeding love that enkindled Thee, O Son of God, willingly to endure such agony for us sinners."

While Francis was kneeling in prayer, there came toward him from heaven a cross. Upon it was the figure of a seraph. It was not the figure of Christ. The face of the crucified figure was beautiful beyond all imagining, though it was the face of suffering.

Two wings were stretched above the seraph's head; two were spread as though for flight; and two wings covered the luminous body. After shining there a moment, it vanished.

The vision was accompanied by such radiance that some muleteers in the vicinity, asleep in a nearby inn, were awakened by the light. Thinking it to be morning, they arose to find instead that a mountain seemed to be burning—flooding the peaks and valleys with light as bright as day.

As Francis remained on his knees pondering the mystery of how it was possible for an immortal spirit to be subject to mortal pangs, the reason was revealed why Divine Providence had shown him the vision in this form. It was that he might understand that it was not by the martyrdom of the body, but by the enkindling of the mind that he must be wholly transformed into the image of Christ crucified.

For Francis, the climax was approaching. Just before daybreak, the stigmata were imprinted upon him . . .

When he came to himself, he was conscious that something extraordinary had happened to him. He looked at his feet and hands. They appeared to be pierced through with nails, the heads of which were in his palms and insteps. Where the points came out on the other side, they were bent over; his finger could be slipped in as into a ring. But the nails seemed to be formed of his own blackened flesh.

He put his hand to his side. From it there came a slow trickle of blood. When he tried to walk, he could not put the soles of his feet to the ground.

Later, Francis was taken down the mountain riding on the donkey, for he was unable to walk. Everywhere people came out to meet him with the cry, "Behold the saint!" Local shepherds had seen the bright light that shone on the mountain sixteen days before and took it to be the sign of some great miracle that had been wrought. They wanted to kiss the saint's hands, which were heavily bandaged.

After that, Francis was very secretive about the stigmata, though this was something difficult to conceal from those with him. He did not like receiving curious visitors. But a few people outside the brotherhood saw the wounds in his hands and feet— among them several cardinals, including the future Pope Alexander IV.

The stigmata has been conferred many times since that day in 1224. There are now over a hundred well-authenticated cases; but this was the first such miracle—with the possible exception of St. Paul the apostle.

In his letter to the Galatians, Paul wrote, "I bear in my body the marks of the Lord Jesus" (Gal. 6:17). The word which is translated "marks" is in the Greek *stigma*. Since Paul used this particular word only here, it is possible that he was the first stigmatic.

After this tremendous spiritual experience, there came upon Francis not only a sense of liberation, but also an energy so vastly increased that he began to make great plans. He felt an immense compassion toward men, for this was what he had asked of God. He went out preaching.

About this time, he encountered a leper who was more than usually surly, though most of these unfortunates were exacting. Francis greeted him, "God give you peace, my brother most dear."

The leper snarled, "What peace may I have from God, who has taken all good from me and left me stinking and rotten?"

The gentle answer came, "My little son, have patience. The infirmities of the body are sent by God for the salvation of the soul, and are of great merit when borne patiently."

But the leper complained again, "How can I bear with patience the pain that racks me day and night? Not only am I afflicted with my disease, but the brothers who are here to do me service, do not serve me as they ought."

"Then my son, I will do the service you need, since you are not content with others."

"What can you do more than others?"

"Whatever it is you wish, that I will do," said the saint.

"Then I wish you to wash me all over, for I stink so vilely that I cannot endure myself."

Francis made hot water and put into it sweet-smelling herbs, and he bathed the ill-tempered leper. As he did so, wherever the fingers of Francis touched, the leprosy departed. The man's soul began to be healed also. His heart melted with compunction for his sins.

It was so great a miracle that Francis had to hurry at once to a distant place to escape the glory that would be given him for so wonderful a thing.

Shortly after that, he found himself very ill. To make matters worse, he was threatened with the loss of his eyesight, having come back from Egypt with a serious eye disease. He would not put himself under medical treatment, but retired to a hut he himself had helped to build beside a convent.

Here, because of swarms of field mice, Francis got no rest. They even climbed upon the table when he was eating. One night he prayed, "Lord, give me help in my infirmities, that I may bear them patiently."

The answer was spoken in his soul, "Tell me, brother, if anyone should give you for these tribulations so great a treasure that the whole world would be nothing, would you not rejoice?"

Francis replied, "I would be content and glad, but I am not worthy of so precious a treasure."

The Voice said, "Rejoice, Francis, for it is the treasure of eternal life which I have laid up for you. From this hour I give it to you, and this affliction is the earnest of that treasure."

From then on Francis had his gladness again, and the nuns would hear him singing as of old the songs he had been accustomed to sing. . . . Still he was not healed.

Finally, after much pressure was placed upon him by others, he put himself in the doctor's hands as an act of religious obedience. But the painful medical treatment did him little good. After seeing another specialist, he had a bad hemorrhage, and it appeared he was about to die. He was afflicted with three other illnesses besides that of the eyes, being troubled with his stomach, spleen, and liver. In addition to this, he had dropsy.

He was taken back to Assisi that he might die there. Carried on a litter, and singing nearly all the time, he approached the city. From the top of a hill, Francis—blind and dying—lifted up his hands and blessed the city he no longer could see.

Francis was placed in the infirmary there, where his suffering became so intense that he told the brothers he would willingly take any kind of martyrdom in exchange. Yet he said, "It has ever been dearest and sweetest and most acceptable to me what my Lord performs in me, to Whose will I desire to be comformable in all things."

Another time he exclaimed, "I give Thee thanks, O Lord God, for all these my pains!" He called his pangs his sisters. They were dear to him. One of the brothers, during the last days, said to him, "Ask God to deal more gently with you, for it seems to me that His hand is laid heavily on you."

Francis responded, "Did I not know that you spoke in simple purity, I would henceforth shun your company; for you have dared to consider the divine counsels concerning me fit for blame."

Struggling out of bed, he kissed the ground, exclaiming, "I thank Thee, O Lord God, for all my pains. I beseech Thee, that if it please Thee, Thou wilt add unto them a hundredfold."

At the very end, his instructions were that he should be laid on the ground in ashes. There he lay with his face uplifted toward heaven, wholly absorbed in God's glory. He asked to be buried in sackcloth in token and example of humility and Lady Poverty.

"Death will be the gate of life to me," he said.

Evening was beginning to fall, and as the 141st Psalm was being sung by the brothers—in which Francis joined in faintly—he received death, still singing. Overhead, a great multitude of larks broke forth into joyous song, as the saint—who loved all of God's creatures—passed to his glory.

"What a shining example of true sainthood!" I exclaimed aloud as I roused myself from the spell of wonder in which the life of Francis had enveloped me. "Such humility . . . such self-denial . . . such obedience to the spiritual ideals he cherished. And what willingness to suffer in a sacrificial way as unto the Lord he loved!"

The voice of my heavenly Companion responded softly, "Truly, the life of this saint was offered up as an evening sacrifice, a sweet-smelling savor; and his prayers ascended as incense before the throne of God."

"No wonder he was counted worthy to bear in his body the marks of the crucified Christ," I murmured.

These thoughts served to remind me of the chapter on vicarious suffering that I had reluctantly written in the first part of the book.

"Lord," I began, "this whole matter of sacrificial suffering and offering is perplexing to all of us. Could I ask You what You wish me to do about the chapter in Part One on that subject?

I didn't want to write it in the first place, but You instructed me to do so. I still don't understand it; and neither does anybody else, apparently. One man asked me if my little lamb, my grand-daughter, died."

"Carmen, you are the one who brought in your grand-daughter," replied my Teacher. "That was the conclusion of *your* logic. We had been talking about Abraham's willingness to sacrifice that which was most dear to him—Isaac, his only son; and of that being a type of the sacrifice of the Son of God."

"You also talked about firstborn and lambs," I reminded Him in an attempt to justify myself. "My little lamb is a very precious firstborn to me, Lord, and she has suffered much in her few short years. Since that chapter was written, more affliction has come her way. An accident, caused by the carelessness of others, lacerated her face and knocked out two front teeth. As a result of this, she will have to wear unsightly braces for several years after her permanent teeth come in. She asked me pitifully, 'Why does everything have to happen to me?' I didn't know what to tell her."

The Spirit replied, "Suffering of any kind is little understood or welcomed by man, and vicarious suffering least of all. Yet both are necessary parts of God's design. Let me ask you a question. When Jesus told His disciples that He must suffer many things, and even be killed, how did Peter react to this?"

"He did an incredibly audacious thing," I answered. "He took Jesus aside and rebuked Him. That has always shocked me. Rebuking Jesus—think of it! He said, 'This must never happen to You!' "

"And what was Jesus' reply?" prompted my Teacher.

"He rebuked Peter in no uncertain terms. 'Get thee behind me, Satan,' Jesus told him. 'You are an offense to me, for you savor not the things of God, but those that are of men' " (Matt. 16:23 AP).

"Peter did not want a crucified Savior," declared the Holy Spirit. "He wanted a conquering King. Israel did not want a suffering Messiah. They saw no comeliness in such a portrait of Him, nothing to be desired in their eyes. They hid as it were their faces from Him, despising Him. They regarded Him as stricken and afflicted by God because of His sins. Yet it was they who caused His suffering; it was for their sins, not His own, that God permitted Him to be smitten. When God freely gave His Son to be the substitute for others, suffering the penalty for their sins, and when Jesus willingly became that substitute, it proved for all eternity the great love of both the Father and the Son."

"But, Lord," I interposed, "Peter loved Jesus. He didn't want Him to suffer and die. How could he help responding from that perfectly natural point of view?"

Said my Teacher, "Peter well represented natural man's heart. The thought of the cross is repugnant to human pride and ambition, as well as to man's love for what is dear to him. The cross too deeply underscores the fact of sin and the need for a blood sacrifice to wash it away.

"Furthermore, it implies the painful and humbling truth that for the disciples, as well as the Master, there must also be a cross. If his Lord is crucified, the disciple must likewise deny himself and take up his cross and follow Him. Jesus died *for* sin. Man must die *to* sin. This is not to man's liking; and therefore the cross always has been, and always will be, unpopular with the world."

When the Spirit finished speaking, I spent a long time meditating on the things He had said. Finally I spoke again.

"Lord, I think I understand a little better now why St. Francis was willing to suffer and give his life as a sacrificial offering to God. It was in humble imitation of the Christ he adored. I can see why he prayed to share His physical pangs—as Francis called them—and to feel the exceedingly great love that 'enkindled' Jesus so that He willingly endured such agony for sinners . . .

"I can better appreciate why the apostle Paul wrote, 'If we be dead with him, we shall also live with him; if we suffer, we shall also reign with him' (II Tim. 2:11,12). Paul was dead to self, the same as St. Francis. That was the only way he could take pleasure in suffering affliction—glorying in it—wearing chains like a criminal, and finally suffering martyrdom for the sake of the Christ Who was put to death for him.

"Peter also came to the place where he was willing—yes, eager—to follow his Lord to death, even death on a cross. He had been so changed, and filled, and empowered by the outpouring of the Holy Spirit that he no longer minded the things of men, but was a partaker of the divine nature in thought and word and deed."

"You have understood correctly, Carmen," replied that same Holy Spirit. "And I desire to pour out My Spirit on all flesh, yours included, for the like purpose of conforming God's children to the image of Christ. That was the reason I introduced the subject of sacrificial suffering. If Jesus could not be perfected without it, how much more needful is it for those who would follow in the path that leads through suffering to glory."

His words brought an unpleasant recollection—the disgraceful way I had reacted to the subject of vicarious suffering. What a clear demonstration I had given of the human nature I partake of! Claiming to be a consecrated firstborn who belongs to those ministering to others, yet plainly lacking a spirit of self-sacrifice . . . jumping to conclusions regarding my granddaughter, conclusions which displayed a total unwillingness to have someone I loved suffer for others . . . in my ignorance and fear crying out, "No, Lord, not my little lamb! This should not happen to her!" All this when the Spirit was beginning to teach an important truth . . .

With a start, I realized I had committed the very same offense that Peter had! I too was mindful of the things of men and self, rather than the things of God. Certainly I showed what a long way I was from being dead to self and alive to God! In fact, I was just the opposite—extremely alive to self, half-dead to God.

"Lord," I confessed with shame, "Forgive me! How far I am from holiness and from the saints I so admire!"

"But you are near to Me," said the Spirit. "Through Me you may partake of the divine nature. And you are not without the chastisement of God, which is for your profit, that you might be a partaker of His holiness."

"Thank You, Lord!" I exclaimed impassionedly. "Thank You for Your discipline, Your training, Your correction of me. I willingly offer to You my whole being—body, soul, and spirit. I even yield to You my love for my little granddaughter, and my desire to spare her from all suffering."

When the Spirit spoke again, His manner was one in which great kindness mingled with authority.

"Carmen, as for your fears regarding certain firstborn, remember that Jesus is the firstborn of many brethren. These firstborn are Mine. They belong to God, and to them belongs the spiritual birthright. Many blessings are promised to the firstborn. Believers who are a part of the church of the firstborn are privileged above all other men.

And, as for your concern for your little lamb, I would remind you that you are not come to Mt. Sinai, which evoked fear even in Moses, and where lambs were for sacrifice and offerings. You are come to Mt. Zion, whereon stands a Lamb; and with Him are those who follow the Lamb whithersoever He goeth. One day you shall come to a holy city, where the Lamb is enthroned, and where His servants behold His face. His name is written in their foreheads, and they shall reign with Him for ever and ever."

XV
"Behold . . . I Will Cure Them"

(Jer. 33:6)

The Bible says, "Worship the Lord in the beauty of holiness" (I Chron. 16:29).

Andrew Murray says, "Humility . . . is the beauty of holiness. Displacement of self by the enthronement of God, a heart so filled with His presence that there is no place for self . . . is humility."

The tombstone of Christina Rossetti says:

"Give me the lowest place: or if for me
That lowest place too high, make one more low
Where I may sit and see
My God and love Thee so."
— (last verse of her poem "The Lowest Place")

"And now, Lord, as the crowning touch of glory to my array of saints, I want to share with others the loveliness of Christina Rossetti."

"Why do you regard her as 'the crowning touch of glory'?" inquired my heavenly Companion.

"Because, to me, she expresses the beauty of holiness in words unexcelled by any writer. Furthermore, her life embodies all the qualities that make a true saint—strength of character, humility, absolute devotion to God, a giving to others in self-sacrifice. When I read her poems—as I do, over and over again—my soul is exalted! What color is to the eye, what music is to the ear, perfume to the nostrils, sweetness to the taste, what velvet is to the touch—all this is the poetry of Christina Rossetti to my spiritual senses. Her exquisite awareness of the beautiful, and particularly of the beauty of God, is like a heavenly balm to my soul."

Christina Rossetti was born in 1830 in London, England (just ten years after Fanny Crosby's birth). She lived to be sixty-four years old; and she was ill most of her days. For the last twenty years of her life, from the age of forty-four on, she was an invalid. But her poems reveal her as a woman who bore suffering bravely and cheerfully.

She began to write poetry in early childhood, and at sixteen she already commanded the quiet flow of language that is like a lullaby to the heart's ear—a gliding tone dropping into silence. In this particular effect, she is incomparable.

One of her best-known poems, composed when she was eighteen, well illustrates this:

> When I am dead, my dearest,
>   Sing no sad songs for me;
> Plant thou no roses at my head,
>   Nor shady cypress tree:
> Be the green grass above me
>   With showers and dewdrops wet;
> And if thou wilt, remember,
>   And if thou wilt, forget.
>
> I shall not see the shadows,
>   I shall not feel the rain;
> I shall not hear the nightingale
>   Sing on, as if in pain:

And dreaming through the twilight
That doth not rise nor set,
Haply I may remember,
And haply may forget.

Though she produced only a few slim volumes of poetry, these made Christina world-famous. Some of her short lyric poems are among the best in English literature. Many have been set to music, and cantatas were composed for two of her longer poems.

A deeply religious person, she was an evangelical Protestant, a regular worshiper in the Anglican Church. (At this point, may I say in passing that should anyone wonder why I have so many "Catholic" saints—the two out of four who were Roman Catholics couldn't have been anything else. In the time of St. Francis and St. Teresa, and in the countries in which they lived, there was no other church. However, I think it is of little importance to God whether a believer is a Catholic or a Protestant. It is rela- tionship to the Lord Jesus Christ, not the church one attends, that makes a saint.)

The first poem I ever read from the pen of Christina Rossetti so impressed me that I inscribed the second verse in the front of my Bible, along with spiritual gems from other sources. These are the lines:

O dream how sweet, too sweet, too bitter-sweet,
Whose wakening should have been in Paradise,
Where souls brimful of love abide and meet;
Where thirsting longing eyes
Watch the slow door
That opening, letting in, lets out no more.

She wrote much about Paradise. In fact, one of her poems bears that title. It begins:

Once in a dream I saw the flowers
That bud and bloom in Paradise . . .

and goes on in that, and in the next verses, to beautifully
describe not only the flowers but the songs of Paradise, the
flowing of the fourfold river, the tree of life, the gate called
Beautiful, the golden streets, the glassy pool, the harps and
crowns of stars, the green palm branches. Completing the poem
is this stanza:

> I hope to see these things again,
>   But not as once in dreams by night;
> To see them with my very sight,
>   And touch and handle and attain:
> To have all Heaven beneath my feet
>   For narrow way that once they trod;
> To have my part with all the saints,
>   And with my God.

Christina's brother, Dante Gabriel, was also a poet, and a
painter of renown as well. It was he who first attempted to get
her work published. He asked an influential friend to submit
Christina's poem "Goblin Market" to a magazine. Outraged by
the metrical irregularities of the verse, the friend flatly declined,
stating, "Your sister should exercise herself in the severest com-
monplace of meter until she can write as the public likes."

To this, Gabriel made the brief remark, "Most senseless, I
think." Posterity has resoundingly endorsed his opinion.

Shortly thereafter, the co-founder of a large publishing house
read another of Christina's poems—"Uphill"—and at once
heralded her as an exciting new poet. He printed this poem in his
magazine, following it with a number of others. I am especially
fond of the opening lines of "Uphill." When I tend to view my
life as one of unceasing toil, these succinct words echo my
feelings:

> Does the road wind up-hill all the way?
>   Yes, to the very end.
> Will the journey take the whole long day?
>   From morn to night, my friend.

Later this same publishing house brought out Christina's first volume of verse. The very poem that had been utterly rejected by Gabriel's influential friend—himself a distinguished writer and critic—was the main attraction. "Goblin Market" was quickly acknowledged as a masterpiece, and brought success and permanent fame to Christina. Her bright day had dawned at last, and she became the object of the adulation bestowed upon genius, assuming the leading position in English letters that she never lost.

"Goblin Market" has many levels of meaning, but on the spiritual level it depicts these truths: To succumb to temptation makes one a victim of that same temptation. Thus man is his own destroyer. . . . The pursuit of earthly pleasure must be renounced if one is to achieve spiritual redemption. . . . Love is a redeemer. An act of sacrificial love on the part of one person in behalf of another results in the latter being saved from spiritual death.

The lengthy and highly descriptive poem tells the story of two sisters—Lizzie and Laura. Both of them heard the cries of goblin merchantmen hawking their tempting, luscious fruits. Lizzie was cautious and full of wise upbraidings about even looking at goblin men; she knew their forbidden fruit would be harmful. But Laura was curious and self-willed. She tasted the evil fruit and then ate her fill.

Afterward, Laura was no longer content with her simple, innocent life. She yearned with a desperation to repeat her experience; and when she could not hear the goblin calls, she gnashed her teeth in balked despair and wept. Her listlessness turned into sickness, and soon she was at the point of death.

Tenderhearted Lizzie so longed to comfort her sister that finally she could stand it no longer. Taking money, she went in search of the goblin men to purchase some of the evil fruit that Laura craved.

When Lizzie found the crafty men, they would not sell her their merchandise but insisted that she eat with them. She steadfastly refused. They pounced upon her, tore her clothes, held her hands and squeezed their fruits against her mouth to make her eat. All their physical assaults were to no avail; she would not open her lips.

Worn out by her resistance, the men departed. When Lizzie reached home, battered and bruised, her face was dripping with juice from the goblin fruit. She offered herself to Laura to kiss.

> "Eat me, drink me, love me;
> Laura, make much of me:
> For your sake I have braved the glen
> And had to do with goblin merchant men."
> Laura started from her chair,
> Flung her arms up in the air,
> Clutched her hair:
> "Lizzie, Lizzie, have you tasted
> For my sake the fruit forbidden?
> Must your light like mine be hidden,
> Your young life like mine be wasted,
> Undone in mine undoing
> And ruined in my ruin,
> Thirsty, cankered, goblin-ridden?"

But when Laura hungrily tasted the juice on her sister's face, her lips began to scorch. It was wormwood to her tongue. She writhed in agony and beat her breast.

> Swift fire spread through her veins, knocked at her heart,
> Met the fire smouldering there
> And overbore its lesser flame;
> She gorged on bitterness without a name.
> Ah! fool, to choose such part
> Of soul-consuming care.

Falling headlong to the floor, both pleasure and anguish past, Laura hung between life and death. All night long Lizzie cared for her. When morning came at last, Laura awoke as from a dream and laughed in the innocent old way, and light danced again in her eyes.

Days, weeks, months, years
Afterwards, when both were wives
With children of their own;
Their mother-hearts beset with fears,
Their lives bound up in tender lives;
Laura would call the little ones
And tell them of her early prime,
Those pleasant days long gone
Of not-returning time:
Would talk about the haunted glen,
The wicked, quaint fruit-merchant men,
Their fruits like honey to the throat,
But poison in the blood;
(Men sell not such in any town;)
Would tell them how her sister stood
In deadly peril to do her good,
And win the fiery antidote:
Then joining hands to little hands
Would bid them cling together,
"For there is no friend like a sister,
In calm or stormy weather,
To cheer one on the tedious way,
To fetch one if one goes astray,
To lift one if one totters down,
To strengthen whilst one stands."

The contrast betweeen human and divine love—the former
transient, like the other beauties of this earth; the latter eternal—
is a recurring theme in Christina's writings. She continually pro-
claims that ultimate satisfaction is only to be found in a more
perfect world beyond:

Lifelong our stumbles, lifelong our regret,
Lifelong our efforts failing and renewed,
While lifelong is our witness, "God is good:"
Who bore with us till now, bears with us yet,
Who still remembers and will not forget,

Who gives us light and warmth and daily food;
  And gracious promises half understood,
And glories half unveiled, whereon to set
Our heart of hearts and eyes of our desire;
  Uplifting us to longing and to love,
Luring us upward from this world of mire,
  Urging us to press on and mount above
  Ourselves and all we have had experience of,
Mounting to Him in love's perpetual fire.

Though Christina fell deeply in love with a man who proved to be unworthy of her, she never married. She loved and was loved, but her heart had early heard the call of God to a dedicated life, to detachment from the things of this world—and to that call she remained true.

Christina's poems have been criticized by some as being too morbid to suit their taste, and at times her language sounds a note of despair rather than hope. Is it any wonder that years of suffering caused her to long for the sleep of death as an escape from intolerable dreariness and weariness? Like St. Francis, she saw death as the gate to eternal life.

Her brother William comments about this:

"Anyone who did not understand that Christina was an almost constant and often sadly smitten invalid, seeing the countenance of Death very close to her own, would form an extremely incorrect notion of her spiritual condition." While she expected an early death, when it did not come, she discontinued her beseeching to be released, and patiently and expectantly finished out her days.

In her poem entitled "From House to Home" she depicts the journey of her soul from earth to heaven, closing with these stanzas:

Beauty for ashes, oil of joy for grief,
  Garment of praise for the spirit of heaviness:
Although today I fade as doth a leaf,
  I languish and grow less . . .

Although today He prunes my twigs with pain,
   Yet doth His blood nourish and warm my root:
Tomorrow I shall put forth buds again,
   And clothe myself with fruit.

Although today I walk in tedious ways,
   Today His staff is turned into a rod,
Yet will I wait for Him the appointed days
   And stay upon my God.

Christina's countenance, with its classical features, so reflected the beauty and serenity of her spirit that she was often asked to pose for religious paintings. When the artist Holman Hunt caught a glimpse of Christina in her early twenties, he immediately requested that she be the model for his head of Christ. The sweetness and gravity of her expression was exactly what he wanted for the Savior's face. The painting, which brought the artist his first public success, turned out to be the celebrated "Light of the World," sometimes called, "Christ at Heart's Door." The famous painting pictures Jesus knocking at the door of the human soul.

Twenty years later, when Christina was forty-one years of age, disease struck—in the form of exophthalmic goiter—marring her lovely countenance and leaving her life in danger. She accepted the affliction with courage and resignation, sustained by her religious faith.

After she recovered from the worst effects of the illness, she gave herself almost completely to devotional prose writings. A book of prayers, religious meditations, and a commentary on the Apocalypse were subsequently published.

During the long dark night of Christina's soul, the Divine Lover's hold on her did not fail, and "through the mists of death, they went hand in hand—beyond sun and moonlight to another land" (to quote loosely lines from her poem "Moonshine").

In common with St. Teresa and St. Francis, Christina's spirit was fired with admiration for that particular manifestation of love for God that is called martyrdom. She expressed this most vividly in a poem that begins:

> Life flows down to death; we cannot bind
>   That current that it should not flee:
> Life flows down to death, as rivers find
>   The inevitable sea. . . .

And ends:

> Sparks fly upward toward their fount of fire,
>   Kindling, flashing, hovering:—
> Kindle, flash, my soul; mount higher and higher
>   Thou whole burnt-offering!

Christina was a self-disciplined and controlled person. As a child, she had a very passionate temper; but her love for her mother and for her Lord enabled her to completely overcome it. In sweetness of resignation to the will of God, she accepted pain, sickness, disfigurement of facial beauty, old age, and death.

> The sweetest blossoms die . . .
>   The youngest blossoms die . . .
> And youth and beauty die.
>   So be it, O my God, Thou God of truth:
>   Better than beauty and than youth
> Are saints and angels, a glad company:
>   And Thou, O Lord, our rest and ease,
>   Art better far than these.

When Christina was physically able, she worked at intervals and for short periods of time in a religious institution called The House of Charity. She became a member of that order, wearing a special habit, and caring for fallen women. For these unfortunates, Christina felt a very deep and divine sympathy. Her heart mourned for them. Many of her best religious poems came forth during these years.

Christina also spent years of her life caring for her ill parents and her two elderly aunts. Whatever her bodily condition, she was always cheerful and ready to listen with genuine interest to others. Visitors frequently came to call, for everyone who met Christina fell under the spell of her intellectual power and attractive personality.

She was the support and comfort of her brother Gabriel in his darkest hours. In the family life of her brother William, she was an influence toward the faith which was her very life and breath. He said of her courage and constancy: "In strength of mind and in devotion to Christ, she continued to maintain an admirable triumph over all physical prostration and suffering."

Christina knew her Bible thoroughly. Her mind was steeped in biblical thought and imagery. Her last book was a book of prose, *The Face of the Deep*. From its treasure, I draw forth a single sentence: "We have heard enough when God ceases to speak, and we have learned enough when we have learned His will."

By the time her mother died, life had gradually stripped Christina of all that she cared for most. She whose heart had long ago turned from earthly attractions to the fadeless glories of the world beyond, was more than ever ready for her own release. But there was a good deal more for her to suffer, and still more to do, before that release came six years later.

Two years prior to her death, Christina underwent surgery for cancer of the breast. The operation was temporarily successful and gave her some months of fairly active life. As long as she had the strength, she steadfastly attended church twice a week, regularly receiving the Sacrament. An atmosphere of serenity and assured peace surrounded her.

The following year, her suffering intensified. With the progression of the illness, pain increased; but her faith and hope in the blessedness toward which she was bound, never wavered. When the end of her journey came, according to the nurse who was on duty, Christina evidently was praying up to five minutes before she died.

"She gave one sigh," reported the nurse, "and in perfect peace at last—left us forever."

At her funeral, a poem of hers—"Lord, Give Us Grace to Mount by Steps of Grace"—set to music especially for the occasion, was sung as an anthem. One biographer brings her account of the life of Christina Rossetti to such a fittingly beautiful conclusion that I repeat it here:

"Unremittingly—through all the years the love of the Divine Lover had overshadowed her, pursued her, checked and urged her, attracted her and won her. For His sake she had battled, renounced, pondered and written, suffered, waited, desired and prayed.

"Beyond earth's clouds awaited her Heavenly Lover."

The hope Christina lived by, and the courage with which she held to it, shine on in the last poem she wrote:

> Heaven overarches earth and sea,
>   Earth sadness and sea bitterness,
> Heaven overarches you and me:
>   A little while and we shall be—
> Please God—where there is no more sea
>   Nor barren wilderness.
>
> Heaven overarches you and me
>   And all earth's gardens and her graves.
> Look up with me until we see
>   The day break and the shadows flee.
> What though tonight wrecks you and me
>   If so tomorrow saves?

XVI
"Neither Shall There Be Any More Pain"

(Rev. 21:4)

I said, "Lord, I know a present-day saint who is a living
example of faith triumphant over repeated physical
suffering and affliction . . . a man of humility, spiritual
maturity, and Christian character."

The Lord said, "I know him too. Interview him
and include it in the book."

The present-day saint said, "When I am going through
a physical demonstration, my body is serving my
spirit, for God has some purpose to accomplish out of
it. . . . He is using this 'trial' as a process."

The interview began with an explosiveness characteristic of
this dynamic man of God. His preaching, not his person, is
explosive—unique in exposition of Scripture, and powerful in
impact.

As a man, he is gentle and lowly in heart—generous and
gracious in manner—a totally dedicated servant of the Lord. He
is gifted with a beautiful singing voice, and when he leads the

congregation in song, I am transported to the very courts of heaven.

From a handful of people, he founded a church—independent of any denominational assistance—whose ministry has spread across the nation, indeed around the world. Numerous television channels have been purchased, over which they broadcast the Gospel, as well as radio stations, foreign and domestic. A Christian day school and a Bible school are also part of their outreach.

But it is not what he has accomplished that most impresses me. It is what he himself is. His humility, goodness, honesty— the faith that he radiates, and his love for God—is so tremendous that secretly I have wished for a blood transfusion from his veins. However, I don't think he could spare it. Not a robust man physically, he has been attacked in the body over and over again. Yet his spirit remains undaunted, and he seems to come back from bouts of suffering stronger spiritually than ever.

We had barely gotten seated in his office when he commenced the interview with these startling words: "I can prove to you that Jesus taught that it was not His will to heal everybody!"

Though I was in perfect agreement with his statement, nevertheless I found myself gasping at the directness of his approach. He went on to say:

"First, let me give you some background about how I came to the realization of this in my own life. About five years ago, I had a tooth pulled. At that time, I was doing heavy physical work, taking outside speaking engagements twice a day, plus the load I was carrying here. When they pulled the tooth, they left a piece of it in the root system. I walked the floor every night for about a week—couldn't sleep at all, I was suffering so. Somebody handed me two tickets to the Hawaiian Islands to take a vacation. I was supposed to leave Saturday. After I had preached Friday night, I was so bad I went home and went to bed. I couldn't get out of bed.

"Sunday morning about four o'clock they took me to the hospital because I was dying, and I knew it. What had happened was that the infection in the tooth had triggered a sugar problem

I had inherited, and if it hadn't been caught right then, I would have died. My sugar count was up over 400, and normal is 120. It had already sent me into shock.

"For eighteen days I lay in that hospital . . .

"Now, all my life I have been rabid for divine healing. I was raised with Smith Wigglesworth and others who were mightily used. Charles Price was a neighbor and a very close friend of mine. My father helped to start Aimee Semple McPherson's Angelus Temple. We followed all their ministries and saw those fabulous days of the supernatural. I was weaned on that. So you couldn't have found a stronger believer in divine healing than I was. I thought God had given us that.

"Yet here I lay in the hospital! I was torn up mentally more than physically, because I kept asking, 'Why?' I had prayed for thousands of people, and they were healed. But here I lay, and I wasn't healed!

"The woman whose ministry is the most outstanding for miracles of healing today, wrote me personal letters assuring me of her prayers. Everyone in this area was praying for me. Still I didn't get better.

"About the fifteenth day, as I was praying, the Lord showed me that this was a spiritual battle more than it was a physical battle. One side issue of what He revealed was that the men who were my doctors—five of them—unconsciously were pleased to manipulate the temple of the Holy Ghost. They were not godly men, and the spirit in them was delighted to keep God under subjection. They were the devil's men—not by dedication, but just because they weren't born of God.

"They had sat around my bed saying, 'You can never preach again.' When the Lord showed me the true picture from the spiritual vantage point, I said, 'I'm going home.'

"From the top supervisor of that hospital on down, they visited my room saying, 'Pastor, that's suicide. We don't have your sugar in balance, and you say you're going out of here?'

" 'Yes sir, I'm going out,' I replied. 'If I have to crawl on my hands and knees, I'm leaving here.'

" 'You can't do that,' they told me. 'We refuse to dismiss you.'

"I said, 'I'm dismissing myself.' On the eighteenth day, I walked out—against all the doctors' orders and against the hospital's recommendation. The minute I walked out, the whole thing began to change for me.

"While I had been lying there, I knew that I would have to come back to my congregation and give some answers that would satisfy them—that would satisfy me. I had continued to cry out unto God, 'Why, Lord, why? What is the real answer?' It was then that the tenth chapter of Luke began to come; and when the Lord was finished, I made my exit from that hospital. This is what He showed me . . .

"The lawyer who came to Jesus asked, 'Master, what must I do to inherit eternal life?' Jesus made the lawyer answer his own question, and that answer was twofold. First, he must love the Lord his God with all his heart, soul, strength, and mind. And secondly, he must love his neighbor as himself. *Both* of these were conditions for eternal life.

"We preach 'Believe on Jesus and you're saved.' But Jesus said that believing *and* loving your neighbor are the conditions for eternal life. The lawyer asked, 'Who is my neighbor?' Now here's where Jesus taught that divine healing wasn't always His will.

"He said that a man went down from Jerusalem to Jericho and fell among thieves—you remember the story. The Levite came along, and the priest, and finally the Samaritan. Note carefully—Jesus did not say the Samaritan was to pray for that man! I can understand how some layman might have said this. But Jesus said the man put oil and wine in his wounds, put him on his own beast, took him to the hospital—in this case, an inn—and said, 'Take care of him. Whatever it costs, hospital bills, etc., when I come back, I'll pay the whole thing.'

"Jesus said, 'That man was a neighbor'—touching a man in his need, and yet not healing him.

"Lying there in the hospital, I looked at myself and I thought, 'I have ministered to that church for over twenty-five years. I have poured out toward the congregation, but they have never known the dimension of being a neighbor to me. I have always been the strong one ministering to them. Now here I am beaten, wrecked and torn, and fallen among thieves.'

"It was then that the situation began to be reversed. They started ministering to me. You can't believe the thousands of cards I received, the tears and the handkerchiefs that were prayed over. People sent flowers and money and came to visit me. In one day, fifty-four visitors came, until the hospital closed the door and put a guard on it to keep people out.

"Well, I hadn't been home from the hospital two weeks, and though I could hardly get out of bed, I said to my wife, 'I'm going to church this morning, and I'm going to preach.'

"They almost carried me in. I stood behind the pulpit, holding on for dear life, and I gave this message from the tenth chapter of Luke. The congregation stood up en masse and ministered back to me when I was so weak I could hardly talk.

"You see, they had caught the meaning of what it says in Colossians 1:24. In that verse, Paul states something that sounds strange to us. He says, in effect, 'I'm making up in my body that which is lacking in the sufferings of Christ, for the sake of His church.'

"For a long time that Scripture bothered me, because I have preached—and you've heard it sung so many times— 'Jesus paid it all; all to Him I owe.' We have the concept that there is nothing that could be added to the dimension of the cross. But there is one thing that God Himself could not bypass being fulfilled, one thing that was lacking in the cross. That was the visible evidence to the present generation of the *power* of the cross.

"I'll say it another way. Jesus, in the time of His crucifixion, was a visible evidence of the mercy of God, and of the ability to suffer in the grace of God for the kingdom of God. Now then, only one generation away, was Paul. He never saw the cross. He never saw how a Man could suffer for the sins of the world, and hang there and cry such things as 'Father, forgive them for they know not what they do!'

"For Paul there was no visible cross. In the literal sense of the word, Calvary visibly was only for that one generation. But

Paul became the visible evidence of the suffering of the cross to the next generation! Remember that he wrote from prison in Rome that there were saints in the household of Caesar who became believers because of his bonds.

"Paul suffered in the flesh, but he could not add anything to the spiritual accomplishment of the cross. Yet he became an all-important visible demonstration of how grace can suffer and still say, 'I glory in my infirmities, that the power of Christ may rest upon me.' "

At this point in the interview, I broke in to ask an important question—one that had been broached by others to me—namely, When I am sick, am I really suffering for Christ? "How do you feel about that?" I queried.

"I could give a dozen illustrations of an affirmative answer to that question," he replied. "Once when I was in the hospital suffering, I was taken out of a ward and put into a semiprivate room with another man. He was a terminal cancer victim. It wasn't long before I found out that he was unsaved. He told me that when he was a little boy, he used to go to a tent meeting, slip under the canvas, and listen to the gospel songs. Those choruses never left him. 'In the Sweet By and By' was one of them.

"I had my little FM radio with me, so one morning when he went into the bathroom, I called our station and asked them to play that particular song on the air and dedicate it to this man. He came out of the bathroom, and the timing was just perfect. All of a sudden, he heard his name on the radio, and the announcer saying, 'We're going to play this song just for you.'

"As the chorus was sung, that man broke down and wept like a baby. 'That brings back my childhood,' he said, 'and what I heard that woman preach in that tent in Chicago.'

"I said to him, 'Man, this is why I'm here—for your sake.'

"Minutes later, he prayed the sinner's prayer and was gloriously saved. You see, the important thing was not that I was sick, for I had already settled with God. But he hadn't. The seed that was planted way back in his childhood needed the proper condition to bear fruit. My sickness provided that condition.

"Another time when I was in the hospital about a year ago, four different people—two backsliders, a nurse, and I can't recall now who the fourth was—turned to God because I lay there. I was unable to figure out why I was there, until I learned it was for their sakes."

"Would you say then that God sent affliction to you for that purpose?" I interjected.

"I wouldn't use the word 'sent,' " he replied. "I think that by directive God allows circumstances to pull us into purposes. For instance, we have a lady who is in the hospital right now. Again. She has more car wrecks than anybody in the church. About every six or eight weeks she has a wreck. Most of the time they're not her fault at all. She will be sitting at a signal waiting for the light to change, and somebody slams into the back of her car and gives her a terrible whiplash, throwing her into the hospital.

"I went to see her. She told me there was a man across the hall who was listening to our radio station. He was almost ninety years old, and was dying of cancer. She asked me if I would talk with him. I did, found out he wasn't saved, and led him to the Lord Jesus Christ. Then I learned that he was the father of a church pastor who had never led his own dad to the Lord—and here he lay there dying!

"When his son met me a few days later, he said, 'I can't thank God enough for bringing you here. I never had the courage to speak to my own dad.' Just a couple of days after the older man was saved, he went on to be with the Lord."

Again I inserted a question. "Do you think it possible that there is a consent in the soul of a person to be willing to suffer for another's good, that perhaps we don't even know about in this life?"

"I would put it a different way" he answered, "and this brings up another verse of Scripture that is seldom spoken about. Acts 5:41 recalls that the apostles, after they had been beaten for preaching about Jesus, rejoiced because they were counted worthy to suffer for His name. That indicates to me that in the infinite wisdom of God, He measures the capacity of a person whether he can suffer and not be defeated. Not everybody is accounted worthy to suffer for Christ,

"Now you take this same lady I was just talking about. Some time ago she called me on the phone and said she was in the hospital. 'I've lost all use of my legs,' she told me. 'It's the strangest thing. They've given me every test in the book, and they can't find out what's the matter with me. They say now that it is probably mentally induced, but they can't figure out why I can't walk.'

"She lay there four or five days. I went down and prayed for her, and God healed her. She walked out of the hospital with no problem whatsoever.

"A few months later, she had an accident again. Back in the hospital she went, wondering, 'What in the world am I here for? I certainly don't deserve it!' And she cried and cried, 'God, why? Why?'

"One day a nurse said to her, 'There's a girl down the hall, a very sweet girl, and she can't walk. Something's wrong with her legs.' This lady said, 'That very same thing happened to me once.' She went down to the other end of the hospital, walked in and ministered to this girl, telling her, 'This happened to me, and the Lord healed me. May I pray for you?'

"She prayed for the girl, left the room, started down the hall. Hearing a commotion of some kind, she turned around—and there was the girl following her down the hall! After that, my friend no longer asked, 'Why, Lord, am I in this hospital?' "

"Do you believe God ever sends diseases upon people?" I put in.

"He can, in His sovereignty; but remember also that He has only to lift His hand of mercy, and the diseases are already there," was his answer. "There was a man in the Bible—Job— who was called 'perfect,' yet he was allowed to be made sick by the will of God."

"Some Christians say that things are not the same as in Job's day," I commented. "They say that it is different since the New

Testament and Calvary. They point to the belief that healing is in the atonement."

To this he responded, "There is no Old and New Testament in the economy of God. That would mean that God changed at Calvary. Way back in Exodus He said, 'I am the Lord that healeth thee.' Christ was the Lamb that was slain before the foundation of the world. So if you tie healing to the atonement, it was the atonement that was made in the economy of God before the world was."

"What is your definition of healing?" I asked.

"True healing is deliverance from the bondage of self-will, deliverance from the spirit of the world, and deliverance from servitude to the flesh. We are such slaves to the body. Jesus was the only person who knew what it was to pre-exist without a body. The body wasn't the great criterion of His life. He knew that if they undressed Him from His body, He would still exist. He could say, 'Take it off; put it on—so what?' We are so wrapped up in the flesh that the minute we get a bellyache, we go to pieces.

"The body should serve the spirit, not the spirit the body. Let me illustrate . . .

"When I was about twenty-three years old, I had a heart attack. I went to the doctors; and after they had given me all the tests, they said that even when I was completely relaxed, my heart was beating as if I were running upstairs—the most strenuous exercise in the world.

"The Lord healed me of that heart trouble when I started preaching. Since then I've worked mixing cement, building buildings, and have done every kind of heavy physical labor.

"One day when we were building the radio towers—it was July, and about 105 in the shade—we were pulling 400-foot cables up the side of a hill, the hardest kind of work, doing it all by hand. I came down the hill in the little pickup truck to get something in the middle of the afternoon, started back up, and had another heart attack.

"My body just folded over the steering wheel. I pulled to the side of the road, and I was gone—just like that. I knew exactly what had happened to me. I said, 'I'll never come out of this one!' Just then the Spirit of the Lord said to me as plain as day, 'Where is the blood?'

"I said, 'Well, Lord, the blood is on the mercy seat, and the blood is on the book, and the blood is on His garments, and the blood is on me.'

"He said, 'That makes you equal with everything that I have shed the blood for.'

"The cry came out of my spirit, 'Satan, look at the blood!'

"Just like an accordion, I was folded up; but instantly I straightened myself up, drove to the top of the hill, and I've never had an attack since. God had superseded the normal processes of life with His life, according to His purpose. Not all healing is that instantaneous, however."

"What is your view regarding gifts of healing?" was my next question.

"Here's where a lot of people get themselves into serious trouble and can't get themselves out of it. They have been taught for years that the ability to heal is a gift; and if you have that gift, you can pray for people and they'll get healed. When God promised the Holy Spirit to the church, He promised the *person* of the Holy Spirit. Not an ability, but the Person.

"You will never find in the New Testament where Peter says, 'I don't have the ability to prophesy—go call John.' You will never hear John say, 'I don't have the gift of healing—go call James.' You'll never hear that. But we preach that. We say one person has the gift of prophecy, one person the gift of miracles, one person the gift of healing, etc. There are gifts of healing—which the Spirit operates through us to accomplish His intended purpose—but not the ability to heal. The healer is God.

"If any one us had the gift of healing, we would heal everybody. Every place we went, we would heal everybody. The gift is in God. But the Holy Spirit has all gifts resident in His person—and you, as His channel, have the potentials of all of them resident in you. You have spoken the word of wisdom thousands of times, but you didn't have it catalogued as such. It just came out of you as the normal demonstration of God."

Later on in the conversation I said to him, "I want to ask you something just as a person, not as a pastor. You have had many physical blows. When you are sick, as you lie on your bed, do you ever wonder, 'Why am I continually laid low? I could be much more effective for Him without this. Why does He let me be stricken again and again?' "

"Well, I would be untruthful if I didn't admit that those questions have come up in my mind. But I am a fatalist in the sense that I believe that the power of God determines and over-rules all events in my life. I am the temple of God. He is more conscious of who I am than I am of myself, because He is altogether conscious. I am very limited in my consciousness. He is altogether knowing, while I am limited in knowledge. So He knows what He is doing with me."

"Then you do not resist these things when they come upon you?" I queried.

"To a degree I do. I'm sure I've eliminated a lot of problems by resisting. From an early age, I was taught to submit to God and to resist the devil. My parents were Pentecostal; I was born in a Pentecostal home. I've never known what it was not to be Pentecostal. My father was not a well-educated man, but he was a powerful man for God. Our home was a constant prayer meeting. We had people coming through there day and night to be prayed for. Miracles were our daily diet, and that's not exaggerating.

"One of my father's favorite sayings was, 'Satan, you're a liar!' I can remember when the flu hit during the first world war. There were perhaps ten or twelve people in our home down with the flu—beds all over the house. My father had taken several of the men who worked for him, and they traveled the city over praying for people with the flu. Then the flu hit him! It would strike instantaneously. One minute you didn't have it—the next minute you did.

"My father weighed about 240 pounds. We lived in an old house that he had built himself—and they didn't brace everything as they do these days. He came stomping in the back door, shouting at the top of his voice, 'Satan, you're a liar!' He shook the house as he stomped past the beds, up the stairs, and into his room. For two hours he walked the floor telling the devil he was a liar. Then he came down again—walked out of the house—and never had any trouble. He had had the flu, but he walked it right out. He wrestled it out. So I know that there are times when we can resist the devil and he will flee."

"But that is not *always* so, is it?" I countered.

"You can turn right around the next time, and it doesn't work that way," he readily acknowledged.

"Do you think that when a saint is attacked—really attacked—that there is a battle in the heavenlies?"

"The Bible says that Satan contended for the body of Moses."

"Also," said I, adding a little more weight to the thought, "the archangel Gabriel who was sent to interpret Daniel's visions, had to fight Satanic angels for three weeks before he could get through. And Daniel himself speaks of being 'sick certain days' after receiving one of these visions" (Dan. 8:27).

"True," he concurred.

"Then what is your feeling about those today who teach that when a believer is not healed, it is because he lacks faith, has sin in his life, or is bound by the devil? They say it is one or the other, or a combination. I don't accept that; do you?"

"It could be any one of them—and it doesn't necessarily have to be any of them. If we say it has to be one of them, what are we going to do about the man where Jesus said neither he nor his parents sinned?"

"There is one more explanation given," I told him. "Others say it is a mental or spiritual block of some kind that keeps a believer from being healed."

"Who can rightly judge whether or not there is a block in another person?" he wisely observed, then went on to say, "There is another side to this entire matter of healing that we don't like even to tolerate. It has to do with the three people that Jesus not only healed, but raised from the dead. We would say these were the biggest miracles in the ministry of Christ. Yet not one of them ever thanked Him, or wrote one Scripture!

"The widow of Nain's son, Jairus' daughter, and Lazarus—

you would have thought that if anybody would have written the Bible, they would. But they never even thanked Him for raising them! There's not a word, not a peep, recorded from their lips. I have an idea that because they had a chance to see the other side, they were disheartened at having to be brought back.

"Another facet that we haven't touched on is old age. Old age is a sickness, a disease, an affliction. But old age also is God's grace to deliver us from this world. If we were always healed, we wouldn't want to leave here. By a simple process originated in divine wisdom, the older we get, the more disenchanted we get because of our inability to relate as we used to."

"That would indicate that we shouldn't *always* pray for healing," I remarked.

"Especially for the very elderly," he agreed. "Even in their weakened condition, it's a torment to be that old, or that weak, or that senile. So God in His sovereignty knows how to divorce us from wanting to be here forever."

"What would you say to those who have hard and fast opinions about divine healing?" I asked.

"Simply this," replied this man of God, who knew whereof he spoke. "Suffering has altered many a rigid opinion. This happened to one of the greatest apostles of faith, who had an outstanding healing ministry—Smith Wigglesworth...

"In one of his services, I saw a woman come to the platform for healing, and the first thing he asked her was, 'Have you got any medicine in your medicine chest?' 'Yes,' she admitted. He picked her up bodily and threw her right off the platform! There was a time when he used that method.

"Another time a pastor took him to a parishioner's home to pray for a sick woman. There were some medicine bottles by her bed. 'Why have you got all that stuff there?' Smith Wigglesworth demanded to know.

"The poor soul attempted to justify herself by reminding him that Paul had a thorn in his flesh and couldn't get deliverance. Wigglesworth sternly rebuked her. 'You are going against Scripture. You are trying to heal the thorn in the flesh by those bottles. You're doubly wrong!' He refused to pray for her. Oh, he was grim!

"Then toward the end of his life, he developed kidney stones. He would lie in bed and hemorrhage all the while, then get up and go preach. They would bring him back and put him to bed, because he couldn't control the hemorrhage. Before he was healed, Brother Wigglesworth became more tolerant. God really taught him through suffering that you just can't demand that everybody always have the victory in answer to prayer."

The last question I posed was this:

"If you had to condense your much experience and wisdom into a nutshell, what would you say to those who are not healed? What would your answer be as to why God does not deliver them?"

"If the person is in the category of being a real saint of God, I would say that the evidence of divine grace in the testimony of suffering is a demonstration to all that God's grace is sufficient. We don't need any grace if we're walking the high hills. We don't need any grace at all. If every part of our body is in perfect health, we don't prove grace. It's in suffering and in opposition that we prove our character—what we really are.

"In the infinite counsel of God, He knows some people just cannot stand suffering. It would tear them apart, and they would give up and deny Him. So I think—now I'm going to say something radical—but I really feel that physical health can be a sign of spiritual weakness! Daniel in the lion's den was a sign of his strength of character. God knew he could take it; some people can't, and so they are not called upon to suffer much of anything.

"I would also say that it is a better gift if one's spiritual problems are discerned and gotten rid of, than if one's physical problems are removed and the other left unhealed. Sometimes, as in the case of Paul and people like Fanny Crosby, it takes the crushing pressure of physical affliction to bring forth the flavor. I wouldn't have planned it that way, but God's ways are not our ways.

"Nevertheless, suffering can perfect character, as in the case of Job. He went through the whole process, and God blessed him more in the end than He did in the beginning because of that suffering. Relationship to God is much more important than healing. The emphasis ought to be more on the truth that we are kept by God, rather than healed by God.

"Now of course all of us would like the premise that anybody at any time in any place can just run to God and get healed. But that's not the way God works. Nor is that faith. Faith is something more than a euphoria, or a sort of halo that you wear and it will do everything any time. God honors faith, but He has a total purpose for each person, and sometimes suffering has a part in that purpose. Christ is for the whole man."

"But regrettably," I sighed, "most people don't want wholeness. They want healing, but they don't want wholeness—or holiness."

"Because they don't want self-denial," he quickly added. "Or sacrifice. Or chastisement. Yet without these, there can be no wholeness, and there can be no true healing."

The interview, which included much more than space permits here, closed with prayer. I particularly cherish one sentence that my present-day saint prayed. It was this: "May those who read this book recognize in its words the wisdom of God; and through those words, may the Holy Spirit speak directly and personally to each reader."

That is my prayer too.

"Well, Lord, we've come to the end of the book. If I weren't so full of joy from being with You, I would probably feel a terrible sadness."

"Why should you be sad?" asked the Holy Spirit.

"Because the sweet fellowship we have had as we've worked together is drawing to a close. I remember how it was before. All of a sudden, You weren't there . . . at least not in the same way."

"I shall still be with you," He answered serenely.

"But I've come to love You so much in this particular way—as my Teacher, daily Companion, Helper, and unfailing Guide. I have *enjoyed* You . . . oh, how much I have enjoyed You! Your presence is the most marvelous pleasure to me. No wonder David said, 'In thy presence is fulness of joy, and at thy right hand are pleasures for evermore' (Ps. 16:11).

"Now I understand what Jesus meant when He prayed for His disciples that 'they might have my joy fulfilled in themselves' (John 15:11 AP). I know why the catechism says that the chief end of man is to glorify God and to *enjoy* Him forever. I want to enjoy You forever, Lord, not just intermittently. Don't leave me or recede from me—please don't! Everything is so tasteless without You."

"Because one purpose has been accomplished—that of writing the book—do you think I have no other purpose to accomplish in you?"

"Oh no, Lord!" I exclaimed. "I just wish I could stay apart with You instead of having to participate in the rat race of this demonized world, and put up with the nastiness and selfishness of mankind. Lord, how can You stand this place? How can You stand us?"

He seemed to smile. "I am not of the world," He said. "Nevertheless, I didn't come to take you out of the world, but to take the world out of you."

I sighed heavily. "Well, I know what that means—back to learning everything the hard way, through suffering and difficulty, instead of through communion and fellowship with You—the easy and blessed way."

"Both ways teach," replied the Spirit. "In each is opportunity for growth in spiritual maturity and character building."

"Lord, this matter of building Christian character...I know that heredity and the actions of others—plus our own choices, thoughts, and reactions—as well as the spirit of the world—all have a great influence on making us what we are. But in the final analysis, isn't it true that our experiences shape our character?"

"And God shapes your experiences," stated my Teacher. "That is even more true."

"Then if our experiences involve physical suffering," I went on thinking out loud, "we just have to trust that the affliction is working out something needful in the soul. God is allowing the suffering in order that healing of another kind may be worked out."

"That is what Paul said," commented the Spirit. " 'Our light affliction, which is but for a moment, works for us a far more exceeding and eternal weight of glory' (II Cor. 4:17AP). Man looks upon suffering as it relates to this present life, and therefore he is continually seeking healing of the body—the outer man. But re-creation of the inner man is what should be sought."

"I noticed, Lord, that my saints were not seeking healing. They were seeking God—to know Him more fully, and to serve Him more perfectly. Each of them needed physical healing, and not a one was physically healed. But all of them were made whole spiritually—and that's far better!"

"What else did you notice about your saints?" my Companion inquired.

"Humility, above all else!" I responded instantly. "In that quality, they were so different from us run-of-the-mill Christians. When I compared myself with them, I was flabbergasted to discover that the very worst sin I have is the one I least suspected—pride."

"Pride has many forms and degrees, and wears many disguises," stated my Teacher. "Nothing is so natural to man, so insidious and hidden from his sight, as pride. Could he but recognize that it has its root and strength in a Satanic power operating outside of him as well as within, man would willingly suffer any humiliation to have it cast out."

"A funny thing, Lord," I observed, "I can plainly see pride manifest in other Christians around me. Why was I blind to it in myself?"

"Because the same sin that is so obnoxious in another, is so comfortable in you," He explained blandly.

"It's all Satan's fault!" I declared. "He breathed pride into man. It's been running in our bloodstream ever since."

"But man in the garden of Eden," pointed out my Teacher, "chose to listen to Satan in direct disobedience to God. Man has been doing that ever since. Yet he has a will of his own, and freedom of choice. Tell me, Carmen, how are you directing your will, and your choices?"

"Don't ask, Lord!" I groaned. "You know that the world and everything in it constantly appeals to self-will and self-choosing. It breeds pride and encourages us to feed it. Pride rules self with a terrible power. Worse than that, it almost seems to *be* our self!"

"It is your self, your human self-nature," said the Spirit bluntly.

With a wave of humiliation, I recalled the glaring example of self and pride that I had displayed in the "Complaint" section of this book. "Lord," I impulsively asked, "did You egg me on to write all those things? What a revelation of self-pity, self-seeking, self-assertion, self-justification, self-indulgence — resentment, bitterness, distorted thinking, dwelling on my own problems instead of abiding in You, fearing for myself and for my loved ones—considering myself to be advanced spiritually over others, yet unwilling to sacrifice myself or what I treasure most! Oh, I can't bear the thought of rereading it! No wonder You told me to let it stand. I would probably tear it up if I tried to edit it. Now I know how Peter must feel when he remembers some of the things that are recorded of him. Why did You let me put all that on paper? What will people think of me?"

"They will think exactly what I told you before—how like you they themselves are," He quietly replied.

"Self has got to go, Lord!" I announced vehemently. "Forget about my prayers for physical healing. I pray to be cured of the sickness that poisons my nature and pollutes the world around me."

At that moment, I was reminded of Webster's definition of the word "cure." I told the Lord, "You know, I can't get over the fact that the dictionary lists 'spiritual charge; care of souls' as the very first meaning of the word 'cure.' I never expected that. But I've come to see for myself that without spiritual wholeness, there is no true healing, regardless of physical improvement or recovery."

"Moreover," added the Spirit, "without spiritual wholeness, there is no true healing even when disease is removed by an act of divine intervention, which men call a miracle."

"Then the only real cure for suffering is spiritual," I concluded. "If we would be made whole, we must yield ourselves completely to God's charge, and commit the care of our souls to Him, keeping our own self-seeking hands off."

"That is the only method of treatment; and it does entail a 'remedy' and a 'process,' as your dictionary states."

"I learned something else from the lives of my saints, Lord," I offered. "Something very essential. There can be no real cure if the human will is not fully submitted to God in unwavering resignation to His divine will. I've heard people say, 'I'm doing the will of God for my life'; but one doesn't have to be around them very long before it is evident that they are doing exactly what they themselves want to do. And they are very unhappy if things don't go to suit them. Their will is anything but yielded. They delight to do their own will, and they call it God's will. The saints were not like that. They accepted whatever came to them, without trying to bend situations and other people to their personal will."

"Carmen, how about your will? Are you ever impatient because things don't go your way? Are you ever self-assertive, self-defensive, touchy, voicing sharp judgments or unkind words? Do you always count others better than yourself?"

I hung my head in shame. "Lord, heal me of those things," I meekly implored.

Then, as is His way, the Holy Spirit introduced something that at first seemed to have no relation to what had preceded it. "There is one more experience I would bring to your remembrance," He said. "It occurred one Sunday evening during a church service, while the congregation was singing 'There Is a River.' Do you remember?"

"I will never forget it, Lord," I answered. "I hope to experience it again—in living reality, not just in vision form."

This particular night, as the strains of that beautiful chorus were being sung over and over—softly, slowly, reverently—I closed my eyes and lost myself in worship and praise. Suddenly I saw the most glorious sight I have ever beheld . . .

It was a room, a throne room, and it was filled with wondrous light—ineffably resplendent. The light was like a Presence, warm and loving, and all-enveloping. Without knowing how I knew, I knew that I was looking into the Holy of Holies in heaven—the place where God Himself dwells.

For just a moment I stood on the threshold, sensing intuitively that if I crossed that invisible boundary line, I would be utterly dissolved. Almighty God does indeed dwell in light unapproachable to man.

The vision lingered for an instant longer, then was gone.

With a sigh that was almost a moan, I opened my eyes and took part in the remainder of the service. But all the while my soul kept pondering the glory of that room, longing to return and enter therein. Yes, to dwell in such a beauteous place forever.

"Were you afraid to enter?" gently inquired the Spirit.

"No, Lord, I was not afraid." Then, hesitatingly, I added, "I was—"

"Yes?" He asked, waiting for me to continue.

"I was not . . . fit . . . to enter."

He made no response to this. My mind began to hear again the refrain of that lovely chorus, "There is a river that flows from deep within; there is a fountain that cleanses from all sin . . . "

After a time, the Holy Spirit spoke, very directly. "Carmen, I am here to make you fit—fit to enter, fit to serve, and fit to abide eternally in the presence of the living God. I am that River—the river that comes from beneath the holiest place in the temple of heaven, and flows outward into the hearts of men. I am that Fountain—the fountain of light and life that wells up within the yielded, consecrated heart."

"Oh Lord," I whispered brokenly, "Flow through me! Cleanse me, flood my whole being with Your life and Your goodness! Take possession of me, and make me over again. From top to bottom, rend me as You rent the veil of the temple. Wrest from me all that is of self, that keeps me from being fit to abide permanently in Your presence."

Came His blessedly assuring reply, "He that hath begun a good work in you will perform it."

Beseechingly, I reached toward Him. "Precious Lord," I cried out in an attempt to voice my inmost yearnings, "for me to be whole, to be holy, I need to be cured of many human sicknesses and diseases that have nothing to do with my physical body! In the complaint section of this book, and of my life, I was all wrapped up in self-centered concerns and fears regarding the flesh. I desired healing, and wondered why I didn't get it. But now things are different. Bodily healing is of little consequence to me; while spiritual wholeness—holiness—is of supreme importance. I want above all else to come and dwell with You, Lord!"

"Then be an imitator of those who have gone on to perfection," counseled my Guide, "those who through perseverance of faith and longsuffering have inherited the promises, and have entered the heavenly rest. A great cloud of these witnesses surrounds you, and waits to welcome you into their company."

"Is that a promise to me that I will arrive?" I asked, falling back into my old routine of seeking reassurance.

"The promise is to you, and to your children, and to all that are afar off, even to as many as God shall call."

"Lord," I said, trying not to sound as though I were protesting, "we could inherit that promise so much more easily without this body! The body is such a drag! We have to give it so much attention; spend so much time, energy, and money just fixing it up and keeping it going—to say nothing of being handicapped and laid low by it over and over again. What a waste!"

"Do not forget," my Teacher reminded me, "the promise includes redemption of the body. That was the first promise I gave to you in the opening chapter of this book—at the beginning of your 'complaint.' I repeat it now as part of your 'cure': 'So when this corruptible shall have put on incorruption, and this mortal shall have put on immortality, then shall be brought to pass the saying that is written, Death is swallowed up in victory' " (I Cor. 15:54).

"But until then, Lord, what can this particular mortal do about her particular corruption?"

"Submit yourself to God, humble yourself in His sight, cleanse yourself from all filthiness of the flesh and spirit. Seek those things that are above, setting your affection on them—not on earthly things. And put on the new nature that I desire to impart to you in righteousness and true holiness."

Struggling to cover up my disappointment that His instructions were not more personal, I made the comment, "All those things are in the Bible, Lord."

"Indeed they are," He responded. "Our task is to get them into you. They have to become more than words in the Bible, and truths which you already believe. They must be made living realities in your daily—hourly—experience. Only then can the will of God become the moving power of your life."

"Lord, with all my imperfections—why did You choose me to write this book?"

"I chose you because you are so average," He said.

"Average!" I echoed in a state of ego-shock. "I thought I was someone special to You, Lord."

"You are," replied the Spirit. "Each of God's children is someone special to Me. You are especially average. As a sufferer, and as a believer, you are average—a middle point between extremes. In some ways, you are above average, in other ways, below; which only makes you all the more average."

Then—out of what I am convinced was sheer kindness—He added, "But you are . . . delightfully . . . average."

After a few moments I said, "Lord, may I ask You three final questions?"

"You may," He consented.

"These questions are not connected in any way. I'll ask the trivial one first. Why is it that—although I am a grandmother—every time I talk with You, I feel and sound like a child?"

"Because you are My child," He replied simply. "More than that, however, you have a childlike spirit. This is essential if one is to be taught. Children are sometimes willful and disobedient, but they are teachable. Unlike many adults, they do not take the position that they know all they need to know. A child's place is to learn, to reverence, and to submit to correction. You, Carmen, happily take that place when we talk together."

"Yet I have thought of our time together as . . . well, I hesitate to say it, but I have called it a 'honeymoon of the Holy Spirit.' Please forgive me, Lord, if in my choice of expression I have offended. I have felt so separated from the world, and so lost in love and wonder and the joy of communion with You that 'honeymoon' is the only word that seems to describe it."

"You have not offended," His gentle answer came. "I would that more who profess to love Me would come apart with Me in a union of spirit with Spirit, that they too might share the joy of holy intimacy."

"I know that in a sense the honeymoon is coming to an end, Lord," I said, my voice reflecting the regret I felt in my heart. "And this brings up my second question, which is more important than the one about feeling like a child . . .

"Some Christians don't understand why I speak of Your coming and visiting with me in such a distinct way, and then seeming to depart. They know that the Holy Spirit indwells all believers from the time of conversion, and they cannot comprehend this transcendent coming and leaving that I have experienced. I try to tell them I know perfectly well that I am never bereft of You, but this has been something extraordinary. You have been present with me—overshadowing me—in a greater measure than I have ever known before. What is a better way to explain this?"

"I have come to reveal Jesus more clearly in you, and through you to others," answered my Teacher. "To each believer, at the time of the new birth, is given a measure of the Spirit. Only to Jesus was the Spirit given without measure. Unto everyone else is given grace according to the measure of the gift of Christ.

"The quickening of the Spirit of Christ within your soul may be termed a 'coming upon,' and the lessening of that power may be regarded as a 'leaving.' But in truth, I never leave you. Sometimes I leave you more on your own, that you might learn through walking in the dark by faith, rather than being led by the hand in the light.

"While we have worked together on the book, for a little while and for a specific purpose, Jesus has taken possession of your soul by His Spirit. Thus you have had a foretaste of that day when He will have complete and constant possession. Then you will have come in the unity of the faith, and in the knowledge of the Son of God, unto perfection, unto the measure of the stature of the fullness of Christ."

"Lord, haste the day!" I cried.

As an afterthought, I said, "I wish all I had to do was work with You. Instead, I have to do so much other work day and night—seven days a week, no holidays, no letup. Customers come in the store and say to me, 'Hello, slave.' Even my husband calls me a workhorse. But I want to be more than just a burdened-down beast 'toiling on'—to quote one of Fanny Crosby's songs. I don't mean to complain, Lord, but I work all the time!"

"So do I," He replied quietly.

"Won't I ever have any rest from my labor?" I entreated.

"Learn what it means to rest in God," instructed my Teacher. "Enter into His rest, and your labor will be easy, your burden light. Let His power work in you. This is the rest of faith." The loving way He said it quelled any further remarks from me.

"What is your third and last question, Carmen?"

"It has to do with sufferers who will be reading this who are in a state of intense physical affliction and distress—perhaps the victims of a fatal disease, incurable, painful, and discouraging.

They are apt to find my puny sufferings contemptible by comparison. My heart goes out to all who suffer in body. I feel a tremendous compassion for them—helpless compassion, I must confess. You look upon them with so much greater love than I, Lord. How does Your heart keep from breaking?"

He answered with infinite tenderness. "It did break, my child. It broke on Calvary. It broke for you, and for all who suffer in this world of suffering. It broke open, that its contents might bring to believers deliverance and redemption, abundant and everlasting life."

"If only we believers would *receive* that life in its fullness!" I burst out. "If the thick crust of carnality that imprisons our soul in self-centeredness could be loosed to set us free! If we would surrender to the Spirit of God instead of to our own willfulness and the spirit of this world, we would experience the goodness of You. It would transform our misery into glory."

After a few moments of silent meditation, and moved by a deep feeling for the suffering of others, I spoke again.

"You know, Lord, speaking of misery—we have a customer who is a pitiful case. Incidentally, she is the wife of a doctor, but medical science can do little to help her. In her late twenties she fell victim to multiple sclerosis, made even more devastating by an automobile accident a few years ago. Confined to a wheelchair, she grows progressively less able to do anything. And she's only in her early thirties!

"For a long time she phoned in the weekly grocery order which we deliver to them. But when her speech became so affected it took almost a solid hour to understand her slow and slurred words, the maid had to take over and give the order. Later we learned that this was the final blow to her self-respect. 'That was the only pleasure left to me,' she told the maid. 'Now even that is taken away.'

"Imagine, Lord, the only pleasure she had in life was telephoning in the grocery order every week! What can we say to that poor soul and to others like her? This is my final question."

With divine sympathy and kindness filling His voice, He

answered, "Every soul must first of all come to Christ for true conversion. Without that, he can receive little from God. But to those who have been born of the Spirit, who sincerely seek to progress beyond the initial stage of salvation—and who are called upon to walk the path of suffering—I would say this:

"Lift your eyes from your pain and defeat and look unto Jesus for the spiritual gift that He has to impart to you. Offer your suffering to Him in a spirit of loving sacrifice, and you will come to recognize the hand of God in it. You may even come to rejoice in your afflictions, to glory in them—*in* them, not *for* them—as the saints before you have done.

"Never let the temporary sufferings of this life rob you of the lasting gain they can effect in the soul. Receive them for what they are—blessed opportunities to die a little more to self, in order that a fuller entrance into fellowship with the suffering, self-denying Savior might be made a reality in you. Suffering, if rightly borne, lays up much treasure in heaven.

"When this is done, God is glorified in the very midst of your fiery trial; and He will reward you with His highest blessing—the privilege of making you partaker not only of His suffering, but of His divine nature, His holiness—the privilege of dwelling in His presence forever."

As I reflected on these words of the Holy Spirit, I was vividly reminded of a person who was an eminent example of the very thing He was saying. Her name was Martha Snell Nicholson . . .

This saint of God suffered almost constantly from her birth in 1899 to her home-going in 1957. Stricken with an incredible number of diseases, she was so crippled by arthritis that she was bedridden most of her life. For thirty years she bore unceasing pain; yet she willfully lived above self-pity. More than that, she triumphed over it, living a victorious Christian life in the face of almost unbearable affliction. She wrote over 900 poems that live on to lift, teach, and bless others.

In one of these poems, which she calls "The Thorn," she speaks of standing as a pauper before the throne of God, begging for one priceless gift to call her own. She took the gift from His hand; but as she departed, she cried, "Lord, this is a thorn, and it has pierced my heart! This is a strange and hurtful gift which You have given me!"

God replied, "I love to give good gifts; I gave my best to thee."

"I took it home," (she wrote) "and though at first

> The cruel thorn hurt sore,
> As long years passed I grew at last
> To love it more and more.
> I learned He never gives a thorn
> Without this added grace:
> He takes the thorn to pin aside
> The veil which hides His face!"

What a wondrous reward for a lesson well-learned . . . The very thing that was so abhorrent to the flesh, God used to reveal His personal presence. Today there is no more thorn, nor crippled, pain-wracked body for Martha Snell Nicholson. She is experiencing the joy which she longingly anticipated in another poem:

Some glad day I shall walk again! Sometime my eager feet
  Sensing a blessed Presence near shall turn and run to meet
The One who, dying on a cross, redeemed my flesh and soul,
  Straightened this twisted spine of mine, and made me new and
    whole!
All memory of helplessness, of crutch, of iron brace
  Will melt like mist when I behold the beauty of His face!
And so I wait. On swift wing comes that blessed moment when
  He'll take my hand, and smiling, teach me how to walk again!

Yes, another of God's saints whose affliction was not removed here, now is made new and whole. From this noble company, who by faith triumphed over the extremities of suffering, we can learn how to bear our lesser trials. From them, we clearly see that God always wills to make whole, but not always to heal physically.

Bodily healing is of minor significance with the Lord. Building faith and trust in Him, in order that strength of character and spiritual maturity may be developed, is His primary aim. Fellowship with Him, unbroken and in all fullness, is His ultimate objective.

From the present-day saint we were given a definition of healing that is worthy of being permanently engraved in the mind of every believer: "True healing is deliverance from the bondage of self-will, deliverance from the spirit of the world, and deliverance from servitude to the flesh."

Divine healing is indeed a reality, but there is no infallible position regarding its manifestations, and no principle that works every time for everybody. All divine healing—whether of body, soul, or spirit—comes through the blood of the Lamb, for the purpose of imparting the endless, imperishable life of Christ into the heart of man.

To the obedient, worshiping soul who faithfully and trustingly yields himself, the Holy Spirit is sent to accomplish this transforming work.

"Lord," I said to Him in adoration and profound gratitude, "thank You for stooping to my level and coming to be with me and in me, that I might someday dwell in Your presence forever. Thank You for making me stronger and better spiritually just by being with You. Thank You for my physical improvement that is so marked I'm almost embarrassed to still include myself with those who are not healed. Though I am not yet whole—nor holy—I am wholly Yours to do with as You will."

"He who wills to make your sanctification perfect and complete, asks no more than that."

So spoke my heavenly Teacher, beloved Companion, blessed Comforter, Helper and Guide—the Spirit of promise, the Spirit of grace, the Spirit of holiness . . . the Spirit of God.